First Philosophy Last Philosophy

First Philosophy Last Philosophy

Western Knowledge Between Metaphysics and the Sciences

Giorgio Agamben

Translated by Zakiya Hanafi

polity

Originally published in Italian as *Filosofia prima filosofia ultima. Il sapere dell'Occidente fra metafisica e scienze* © 2023 Giulio Einaudi editore s.p.a., Torino

This English edition © Polity Press, 2024

The translation of this work has been funded by SEPS
Segretariato Europeo per le Pubblicazioni Scientifiche

Via Val d'Aposa 7 – 40123 Bologna – Italy
seps@seps.it – www.seps.it

This book has been translated thanks to a translation grant awarded by the Italian
Ministry of Foreign Affairs and International Cooperation / Questo libro è stato
tradotto grazie a un contributo alla traduzione assegnato dal Ministero degli Affari
Esteri e della Cooperazione Internazionale italiano.

Polity Press
65 Bridge Street
Cambridge CB2 1UR, UK

Polity Press
111 River Street
Hoboken, NJ 07030, USA

Library of Congress Control Number: 2023946010

ISBN-13: 978-1-5095-6051-6 – hardback
ISBN-13: 978-1-5095-6052-3 – paperback

A catalogue record for this book is available from the British Library.

Typeset in 11 on 14 pt Sabon
by Cheshire Typesetting Ltd, Cuddington, Cheshire
Printed and bound in Great Britain by CPI Group (UK) Ltd, Croydon

The publisher has used its best endeavours to ensure that the URLs for external
websites referred to in this book are correct and active at the time of going to press.
However, the publisher has no responsibility for the websites and can make no
guarantee that a site will remain live or that the content is or will remain appropriate.

Every effort has been made to trace all copyright holders, but if any have been
overlooked the publisher will be pleased to include any necessary credits in any
subsequent reprint or edition.

For further information on Polity, visit our website:
politybooks.com

Contents

Thus, the whole of philosophy is like a tree. The roots are metaphysics, the trunk is physics, and the branches emerging from the trunk are all the other sciences.

René Descartes

Therefore, our regeneration depends upon what one might call an "overphilosophy," which, knowing things completely and profoundly, brings us closer to nature.

Giacomo Leopardi

Translator's Note

Italian has more options for expressing "being" than English: *essere, ente, esistente*. This multiplicity is amplified by the Greek and German equivalents, especially in the tradition of Heidegger translations, which expand the English-language option with "Being," "beings," "the being," and even "beying." Readers who are interested in this intriguing topic (a Borgesian hall of mirrors or labyrinth or rabbit hole, depending on your aesthetic) are invited to read Umberto Eco's chapter "On Being" in *Kant and the Platypus: Essays on Language and Cognition* (trans. Alastair McEwen, San Diego, Harcourt, 1997, pp. 9–56). Initially I considered retaining the distinctiveness of *l'ente in quanto ente, l'essere in quanto essere*, and *l'esistente in quanto esistente*, for example, by using respectively "the being insofar as it is a being," "being as being," and "the existent considered as existent." In private correspondence, however, Agamben stated that the Italian distinctions he makes in this book between *essere, ente*, and *esistente* are not pertinent. Therefore, on the basis of the majority of

English translations of the texts cited, I have chosen to use the phrase "being qua being" to translate all these locutions, unless the distinction seems significant in a particular context. In the Heidegger quotations, for example, I retain "Being" with a capital B, since to use the lowercase "being" would annul the ontological difference signaled by "Being" versus "beings" and create confusion for readers who are familiar with this usage.

I took a similarly ecumenical approach to translating the citations from ancient Greek and Latin, the majority of which are translated into Italian by Agamben himself. The notes and the bibliography list the foreign-language sources cited in the original Italian text and provide English editions, when available. For Aristotle, I based my terminology primarily on the revised Oxford translation of *The Complete Works of Aristotle*, edited by Jonathan Barnes in the Bollingen Series (Princeton, NJ, Princeton University Press, 1984, Bollingen Series 71, Part 2). Nevertheless, my English translations of all cited passages are based on the author's Italian renditions, supplemented and modified according to the corresponding English editions, when available. It should be noted, then, that even when English editions are cited, priority is always given to preserving the intention and lexical consistency of the original Italian version.

This translation benefited greatly from the vital editing and research work of Manuela Tecusan, who also corrected and completed the quotations from ancient Greek and Latin sources. My thanks also go to Kevin Attell, who reviewed the first draft and offered insightful comments.

Zakiya Hanafi
Seattle, 2023

I

Second Philosophy

1. This study investigates what the western philosophical tradition has intended by the expression "first philosophy," which this same tradition, or at least a large part of it, has also called by the name of "metaphysics." My interest here is not so much to set out a theoretical definition as to understand the strategic role this concept has played in the history of philosophy. My hypothesis is that the possibility or impossibility of a first philosophy (or metaphysics) determines the fate of every practical philosophy – in the sense, for example, that the impossibility of a first philosophy since Kant is said to define the status of modern thought[1] and, conversely, that the possibility of a metaphysics is said to define the status of classical philosophy up to Kant. Even if what "first philosophy" designates turns out to have no object in the end and the primordiality it claims proves to be entirely baseless, this would not make its function any less crucial: because at stake is nothing less than the definition – in the strict sense of setting boundaries – of philosophy in relation to other forms of

knowledge and vice versa. In this sense, first philosophy is in truth a second or last philosophy, which presupposes and accompanies the knowledge that belongs to other disciplines, particularly the physical and mathematical sciences. At issue in first philosophy, then – such is my further hypothesis – is the relationship of domination or subservience, and possibly conflict, between philosophy and science in western culture.

As for the term "metaphysics," Luc Brisson has shown that, although historians of philosophy use it as if it named a field already established at the beginning of western philosophy, in no way does the word appear in classical Greek. Starting from Nicholas of Damascus (first half of the first century CE), the expression *ta meta ta phusika* begins to appear, but only to designate Aristotle's treatises. Paul Moraux has demonstrated, however, that the traditionally held meaning of "writings that follow those on physics" is inaccurate: on the list of works by Aristotle that he reconstructs, physics is followed instead by mathematics. Starting with Aristotle's ancient commentators, then, the title *ta meta ta phusika* also defines the particular dignity of the science (first philosophy) that deals with forms that exist separately from matter ("But as much of [this science] as is concerned with forms entirely separated from matter, and with the pure activity of the actual intellect, this they [the Peripatetics] call 'theological' and 'first philosophy' and 'metaphysics', as referring to what is found beyond physical realities"[2]) and comes after physics in the order of knowledge ("The science sought and presented here is wisdom or theology, to which he [Aristotle] also gives the title *ta meta ta phusika*, because, from our point of view, it comes in order after physics"[3]). In any case, the syntagm is certainly not Aristotle's. In two passages (*On the Heavens*, 277b10 and *Movement of Animals* 700b7) he seems to use instead the title *ta peri tēs prōtēs philosophias* ("about first philosophy" or "about first principles"), presumably in reference to the theological treatise of Book Λ (Lambda = 12). The term "metaphysics," which we use to refer to a work by

------

Aristotle as well as to the illustrious form of philosophy, derives from the medieval Latin traditions of Aristotle's treatise and is therefore relatively late. From scholasticism on, "metaphysics" tends to overlap with the syntagm "first philosophy," and it is significant that, in a letter written to Mersenne in December 1640, Descartes refers to his *Meditations on First Philosophy* as "my Metaphysics."

2. Because "first philosophy" (*prōtē philosophia*) appears in Aristotle seven times,[4] an examination of the relevant passages is a necessary premise to any interpretation of the concept.

It has been noted that, at the points where first philosophy appears in the *Metaphysics*, the demarcating function it performs vis-à-vis the other theoretical sciences – the physical sciences and mathematics – is particularly evident.[5] In Book E (Epsilon = 6), Aristotle begins by distinguishing, among the theoretical sciences, physics and mathematics, which together "mark off" (*perigrapsamenai*) "a certain being and a certain genus" (*on ti kai genos ti*) and do not deal "with being simply or with being qua being or with the what-it-is" (*peri ontos haplōs oude hēi on oude tou ti estin*) (1025b9–10). "That physics is a theoretical [*theōrētikē*] [science]," he continues, "is plain from these considerations. Mathematics is also theoretical; but whether it deals with things that are immovable and separable [*akinētōn kai chōristōn*] from matter is not at present clear, although it studies some *mathēmata* insofar as they are immovable and separable. But if there is something that is eternal and immovable and separable, it is clear that knowledge of it belongs to a theoretical science – not, however, to physics (for physics deals with movable things) nor to mathematics, but to a science prior [*proteras*] to both. For physics deals with things that are separable from matter but not immovable, and some parts of mathematics deal with things that are immovable and inseparable, but embodied in matter; while the first [science] deals with things that are both separable and immovable. Now all causes [*panta ta aitia*] must be eternal, but especially these. For they are the causes of the divine things that are manifest [*tois phanerois*]. There must, then, be three theoretical philosophies [*philosophiai theōrētikai*], mathematics, physics, and theology [*theologikē*], since it is quite obvious indeed that if the divine exists anywhere, it exists in a nature of this sort. And the most honorable [*timiōtatēn*] philosophy must be concerned with the most honorable genus. The theoretical sciences must be preferred to the other sciences, and this to the other theoretical sciences. One might raise the question whether first philosophy is universal [*katholou*] or deals with a certain genus or one certain nature; for not even the mathematical sciences are all alike in this respect, since geometry and astronomy deal with a certain nature, while universal mathematics applies alike to all. If there is no other existence [*tis hetera ousia*] along with those composed by nature, physics would be the first science [*prōtē epistēmē*]; but if there is an immovable existence, this is prior [*protera*] and the philosophy will be first [*prōtē*] and universal in this way, because it is first. And it will contemplate being qua being, both the what-it-is and that which inheres in it qua being." (1026a7–33)

A glancing examination of how the text is structured and the way the argumentation unfolds shows that first philosophy is always mentioned in relation to some limitation of the other two "theoretical philosophies,"

---

especially physics or natural science [*phusikē*], which without first philosophy "would be the primary science." From the beginning, as has been suggested, what is in question is not the definition of first philosophy as much as a "strategy of secondarization" of physics.[6] As Aristotle points out on two occasions, philosophy is not primary (*prōtē*), it is simply prior (*protera*): it is defined not absolutely but comparatively (*protera* is a comparative formed on *pro*).

This also holds for the definition (or rather lack of definition) of first philosophy's object, which is invariably found in relation to those of physics and mathematics, almost as if the regionalization of being ("a certain being and a certain genus," *on ti kai genos ti*) it implies were to result from subtraction from or complication of a generic being, characterized as simple (*haplōs*, without folds). As a definition of first philosophy's object, the formula "being qua being" (*on hēi on*) would be vacuous and generic, were it not contrasted with the *ti* of physics. Even when the qualifiers "immovable and separable" are used to specify the object, they acquire their meaning through opposition to "movable and separable" and "immovable and inseparable," which define the objects of the other two sciences. And it is significant that the reality of an immovable existence is expressed hypothetically (*ei d'esti tis ousia akinētos*, "if there is some immovable existence"). The further qualification of the object as "divine" in this text seems so inconsistent with the initial reference to "being qua being" that Natorp and Jaeger came to the rash conclusion that the definition of first philosophy in Aristotle is twofold and contradictory, because it claims to bundle ontology (being qua being) together with theology

5

(which refers to the discussion on the immovable mover in Book Λ (12)).

Taking up Léon Robin's suggestion,[7] every time the context seems to require it, I prefer to translate *ousia* with "existence" rather than "substance" – not simply to preserve its etymological connection with *on* (being) and *einai* (to be), but also because the translation "substance," which Boethius transmitted to western philosophy, leads to identifying *ousia* with *hupokeimenon*, the "lying under," which goes against Aristotle's explicit intention.

Natorp, in his 1888 article "Thema und Disposition der aristotelischen Metaphysik," defines Aristotle's *Metaphysics* not only as a "torso," insofar as it is fragmentary and incomplete, but also as implying an "unacceptable contradiction" [*unleidlicher Widerspruch*][8] between a general determination of the object of first philosophy as *haplōs* being and a determination of it as a "determinate field of being" (in the final analysis, the immovable and immaterial *ousia* of theology). According to Natorp, the discussion in Book E, a discussion that tries to reconcile heterogeneous concepts and for this reason strikes him as an interpolation, "results in the fact that the fundamental philosophical science is defined on the one hand as the science that deals with being in general and, on the other, as the science that at the same time has a particular object, namely the immovable and immaterial substance. We have yet to fully grasp that this equivocal (*doppelsinnige*, "with two meanings") notion of the task of *prōtē philosophia* entails an unacceptable contradiction, since *on haplōs* or *on hēi on* and *on ti kai genos ti* are contrary and mutually exclusive. A science that deals with being in general qua being must be superordinate to all those that deal with a particular field; it cannot at the same time coincide with one of them, even if that field were also the most important and illustrious of them all."[9]

Similarly, many decades later, Pierre Aubenque distinguished in Aristotle's text between a science of being qua being, which does not coincide with first philosophy, and theology, which concerns the eternal and immovable substance.[10]

We will return to this alleged duality of the object of first philosophy, as it has a long lineage in the history of philosophy.

3. At *Metaphysics* 1061b19ff., in Book K (Kappa = 11), the strategy is the same – and so, too, in the following passage of the same book (1064a30ff.). Aristotle seeks to show that there is only one science, philosophy, that deals with being qua being, whereas physics studies beings not insofar as they are beings but insofar as they partake of motion, and mathematics insofar as they represent a certain quantity. "Since even the mathematician uses the common notions only in a particular sense, it must be the business of primary philosophy to examine the principles of mathematics also. [. . .] [M]athematics marks off a part of its proper subject matter and produces theoretical knowledge about this part, for example, about lines or angles or numbers or some other sort of quantity – not, however, as beings, but only insofar as each of them is continuous in one or two or three dimensions. Philosophy by contrast does not investigate particular things insofar as each of them has a certain attribute but contemplates [*theōrei*] being qua being in each of them. Physics is in the same position as mathematics; for physics studies the attributes and causes of things insofar as they move and not insofar as they are, whereas, as we have said, it is the province of the first science to deal with these things only insofar as their subject is, and not in virtue of any other aspect. We must therefore posit the thesis that both physics and mathematics are parts of wisdom [*merē tēs sophias*]."

It is clear that the formula "being qua being" serves here essentially to limit the object of physics and mathematics. Given that its topic cannot be the object of the other two theoretical sciences, first philosophy (significantly, called "wisdom" here, and not *epistēmē*) is what on the one hand remains after this subtraction and on the other hand defines its unity only by placing the other two as its parts.

4. The opposition to physics is equally marked in the two passages of Aristotle's *Physics*. In the first (192a35–36), which comes after a polemic with the Platonists, he seems to hint fleetingly at a definition of first philosophy's task: "The accurate determination of the first principle in terms of form [*peri de tēs kata to eidos archēs*], whether it is one or many and what it is or what they are, is the task of first philosophy; so it may be set aside until the appropriate time comes for that. But as for the natural and perishable forms, we shall discuss them further on." Here, too, the vague expression "the first principle in terms of form" acquires specificity through opposition to the "natural and perishable forms" that are the object of physical science.

The aim of placing limits in relation to natural science is even clearer in the second passage (194b14–15), which starts by asking: "to what point [*mechri de posou*] then must the student of nature know the form and the what-it-is? Up to a point, perhaps, as the doctor must know sinew or the smith bronze, that is, until he understands the purpose of each [*tinos . . . heneka*]. He [the student of nature] is concerned only with things whose forms are separable but do not exist apart from matter, for humans are begotten by humans and by the sun as well. But how things stand for the separable and what it is, defining it is the task [*ergon*] of first philosophy." The function of first philosophy corresponds here to placing a limit ("to what point") on the physicist's work. If the natural scientist can know only a *ti*, a certain thing, then the philosopher must know a non-*ti*, an indeterminate thing.

5. In the passage of *On the Soul*, the inquiry concerns the affections (or impressions) of the soul – anger, tenderness, fear, hate, and so on – which are forms contained in a material (in a particular body). For this reason, they are the province of physics, which deals not with form alone or matter alone, but with form insofar as it is in a particular material. "Which [. . .] then, is the physicist? The one who speaks of the material, ignoring the form? Or the one who speaks only of the form? Is it not rather the one who combines both? [. . .] Certainly it is not only one who concerns himself with the inseparable and separable affections. The physicist concerns himself with all the workings and affections insofar as they belong to a certain material, whereas whatever is not of this character he leaves to others, in certain cases it may be to a specialist, such as a carpenter or a doctor. Affections that are inseparable and are considered by abstraction as not belonging to a certain body are the concern of the mathematician. And insofar as they are instead separable, that is the concern of the first philosopher [*ho prōtos philosophos*]." (403b7–16)

The mutual intertwining between the definition of the first philosopher and that of the physicist, the mathematician, and the craftsman is so imbricated here that they cannot possibly be considered in isolation. And it is certainly no accident that the definition of first philosophy's object comes last: in the words of Alexander of Aphrodisias, it can come "in order" only "after physics."

6. In *On the Heavens* (277 b9–11), first philosophy intervenes not only to demarcate itself from physics, which, according to the earlier pages, deals with the single heaven and its movement, but also to validate the arguments of physics: "Further, it [that there is a unique heaven] might also be shown by means of the arguments drawn from first philosophy and from the circular motion, which is necessarily eternal, both here and in other worlds as well." It goes without saying, however, that the arguments in question, which are in no way specified, can incorporate the physicists' arguments precisely because they are assumed to be defined as heterogeneous, even if only in relation to them.

7. Luc Brisson has noted that, in the passage from *Movement of Animals*, namely 700b4–11, first philosophy appears to be mentioned as the title of a treatise: *en tois peri tēs prōtēs philosophias*, "in the [writings or discourses] about first philosophy."[11] In any case, here, too, the object of first philosophy is defined in opposition to those that "remain to be investigated" after it: "Now whether the soul is moved or not, and how it is moved if it be moved, has been stated before in our treatise concerning it. And since all inanimate things are moved by some other thing – and the manner of the movement of the first and eternally moved, and how the first mover moves it, has been determined before in our [writings or discourses] on first philosophy, it remains to investigate [*loipon esti theōrēsai*] how the soul moves the body and what the origin of movement is in a living creature."

The task of first philosophy – to investigate the prime mover – implies the task of a second philosophy – to investigate the movement of living creatures.

8. The idea of a second philosophy is contained in a passage in *Metaphysics*, Book Γ (Gamma = 4), namely 1004a3–4, which elliptically but clearly evokes a first philosophy: "And there are as many parts [*merē*] of philosophy as there are existences [*ousiai*]; so that there must necessarily be among them a first [philosophy] and one that follows this [*einai tina prōtēn kai echomenēn autōn*] [. . .] 'Philosopher' is like 'mathematician,' for mathematics also has parts, and there is a first and a second science and other successive ones within the sphere of mathematics." First philosophy presupposes necessarily a second philosophy and exists only to the extent that it, too, exists.

In a passage a little further on (1005a33–1005b2), Aristotle adds in the same vein: "But since there is a philosopher who is above [*anōterō*] the physicist [. . .], research on these matters will belong to the theorist who studies the universal and the first existence. Physics also is a kind of wisdom [*sophia*], but it is not the first kind."

The expression *on hēi on*, "being qua being," is technically Aristotelian. Plato uses instead the phrase *ontōs* or *alēthōs on*, "that which really is," in a similar sense. Translating the adverb *ontōs* is not easy, but rendering it with "really," as is usually done, as if to emphasize objective reality, is certainly not accurate. In the *Phaedrus*, where the expression occurs several times, *ousia ontōs ousa* is colorless and formless, and yet there is true science and knowledge in it (an "*epistēmē* that is in that which is *ontōs on*," 247e1). In the *Seventh Letter*, the "fifth" that is dear to Plato's heart, defined as "the thing that (or the thing through which something) is knowable and truly existing" (*gnōston te kai alēthōs estin on*), can be reached only by passing through the other four: the name, the definition (discourse, *logos*), the sensible being (the image), and the knowledge (science, *epistēmē*). Aristotle likely intended to clarify his teacher's term by dissolving the adverb *ontōs* into the repetition "qua being." In any case, what is important to Aristotle is not only knowability but above all *haplōs* existence, the pure fact of something's being, independently of its particular properties. From Plato's list he extracts the third, the sensible object, and takes it in its pure existence, independently of its properties; at the same time he eliminates the fifth (the idea) as unnecessary duplication. Being qua being is a sort of contraction of the third and the fifth on Plato's list.

9. Investigation into the concept of first philosophy was thrown off course by Augustin Mansion's extensive study of the problem in 1958. The very wording of the book's topic – whether it is possible to identify first philosophy with metaphysics in Aristotle's thought – is vitiated by a singular anachronism, for it compares a concept that the philosopher uses multiple times with a word that, as we have seen, simply does not exist in the Aristotelian lexicon. It is surprising, to say the least, that Mansion cites "several passages in which metaphysics and the metaphysical are at issue" in Aristotle's writings,[12] without realizing that, by doing so, he is following a habit, unfortunately not infrequent among historians of philosophy, of projecting onto the text under his interpretation a concept that was developed many centuries later. The fact is that Mansion transforms into systematic categories the chronological distinction that, in a study he duly cites, Jaeger already established (and so had Natorp before him) between the different conceptions that Aristotle had endorsed as his thought evolved: on the one hand, first philosophy, whose object is none

other than the supersensible; and, on the other, meta-physics as the science of being qua being.

According to Mansion, in Book E Aristotle defines first philosophy primarily as a science of the separable and the immovable, whose object par excellence is God. However, since a few lines further down he conceives of it as a universal science, he has no choice but to lead it back to metaphysics, "basing himself on the consideration that first philosophy, having the absolutely first being as its object, must provide the ultimate explanation for all that is. At this point first philosophy, the science of the immaterial, is taken up to some extent into the metaphysics of being qua being. It is perhaps out of a scruple for unity that Aristotle affirms unrestrictedly, but at the expense of precision and rigor, that first philosophy is also the fully universal philosophical science."[13]

10.   A simple rereading of the passage in Book E shows that Mansion's thesis has no philological basis. In no way does Aristotle distinguish first philosophy from metaphysics; in fact he starts by defining it by contrast to mathematics and physics, which deal with "a certain being and a certain genus" (*on ti kai genos ti*), since first philosophy studies rather "*haplōs* being and being qua being" (1025b9–10). In other words, at issue are two ways of considering the object's existence: one time as a certain being with its properties, another time *haplōs*, absolutely. The contiguity here between *on haplōs* and *on hēi on* is crucial: to consider a being qua being means to consider it absolutely, with no reference to its particular attributes. "Philosophy," he would go on to write in the passage cited from Book K, "does not investigate

particular things insofar as each of them has a certain attribute but in each of them contemplates being qua being." For this reason, since *on hēi on* is not another object but is "each object" considered *haplōs*, in its pure existence, without any other ontological determination, it can be defined as universal and divine (in 1001a23, *on* is defined, together with *hen*, as "the most universal term of all," *katholou malista pantōn*). To think of a being qua being means in this sense to think of a first and absolute existence, and the "philosophy will be first [*prōtē*] and universal in this way, because it is first. And it will contemplate being qua being, both the what-it-is and what inheres in it qua being" (1026a7–33). Accordingly, for Aristotle, defining *on hēi on* as divine did not in any way mean transforming it into a particular being.

What Natorp apparently fails to understand is that, for Aristotle (and for the ancient Greek mentality in general), there is no "unacceptable contradiction" between the *on haplōs* and the *theion*, and that the god in Book Λ is not an *on ti kai genos ti*. If such a *haplos* substance is defined as separable and immovable, it is because only a substance that is separable both from matter and from movement can be simple and universal, that is, subtracted from the particularity of the objects of natural science and mathematics. Contrary to what modern scholars think, there is no opposition between separable and immovable being (the object of first philosophy or theology) and being qua being, the object of a metaphysics that for Aristotle simply did not exist. The object of first philosophy is not the split between ontology and theology: at issue is only a distinction and, along with it, an articulation between first philosophy and the other two theoretical sciences, physics and mathematics.

For this reason, Aristotle can claim that his task is to ask the question "that was sought of old, at present, and always" (*to palai te kai nun kai aei zētoumenon*) and "that always leads us into a dead-end" (*aei aporoumenon – aporia* being literally the absence of a way): "what is being" (*ti to on*)?" (1028b3–4); and he can answer *ousia*, pure existence. And yet *ousia*, "through which each existent exists," is once again defined negatively, by not being a *ti on* – a certain particular being, the object of physics and mathematics – but an absolute existent (*ou ti on all'on haplōs hē ousia an eiē*, 1028a30).

Avicenna understands perfectly that there is no contradiction between asserting that the subject of metaphysics is the existent as such and at the same time defining it as "divine science"; he writes that "often things are named after their noblest meaning, their noblest part, and the part which is akin to their purpose. It would thus be as if this [metaphysical] science is the one whose perfection, noblest part, and primary purpose was knowledge of what is separable from nature in every respect [that is, God and the separable substances]."[14] Equally clear in Avicenna is his awareness of the connection that links first philosophy to mathematics, physics, and the other particular sciences: "Hence, the benefit of this science [metaphysics] [. . .] is to bestow certainty on the principles of the particular sciences and to validate the quiddity of the things they share in common."[15] But the relationship between metaphysics and the sciences is anything but simple. This is evident from Avicenna's realization that there could be a vicious circle in it, since, as he explains, the study of physics and mathematics precedes that of metaphysics. "A questioner, however, may ask and say: 'If the principles in the natural sciences and mathematics are only demonstrated in this science, and [if] the questions in [those] two sciences are demonstrated through the principles, and [if] the principles of those two sciences become principles for this [metaphysical] science, this would be a circular demonstration, becoming, in the final analysis, a demonstration of a thing from itself.'"[16]

For this reason, Avicenna must concede that the principles of mathematics and physics are evident in themselves and, in this sense, have no internal need for further demonstration through metaphysics. "Thus, in its own right, this science should be prior to all the [other] sciences; but, from our point of view, it is posterior to all of them." And yet, even if its name describes it as "that which is after nature (*ma ba'd al-tabi'a*), if considered in itself, it deserves to be named "the science of what is prior to nature."[17]

We do well to clear the field of the misunderstandings created by the acritical projection of Judeo-Christian concepts of God and theology onto Aristotle's theological science. Elementary philological caution shows that Aristotle prefers the adjective *theion*, which appears much more often, to the noun *theos*; significantly, he also uses it in the comparative and superlative forms and in the adverbial form.[18] Heidegger's assertion that first philosophy would be more accurately called "theiology" than "theology"[19] also applies to Aristotle's theological science: there is no theology in Aristotle, only a theiology. After all, Aristotle does not use the word *theologia*. He limits himself to calling the science in question *theologikē*, an adjective that implies a "technical–scientific meaning."[20] Even when named as god, *theos* does not designate the supreme entity of a monotheistic theology, but an apposition or predicate that serves to mark the excellence of the *ousia prōtē* and of the *on haplōs*. In *On the Heavens* (270b5–10), when describing the heavens as the primary *ousia* of all, he calls it most divine, because humans, "whether barbarian or Greek, assign the highest place to the divine." That the divine is simply the adjective best suited to the primary *ousia* is stated beyond any doubt in the passage in Book Λ (1074b1ff.) in which Aristotle, after stating that "the divine encompasses the whole of nature," brings in the mythical tales in which the gods have human form and adds: "But if we leave these tales aside and take only the first, namely that they thought that the primary *ousiai* were gods, we would have to regard it as divinely said." With good reason, then, in his 1926 course titled *Basic Concepts of*

Ancient Philosophy, Heidegger wrote that *theion* in Aristotle has "nothing to do with religiosity" but is "a *neutral, ontological* concept."[21] It is significant that the word "god" appears for the first time in *Metaphysics* in connection with the "most divine" science, which investigates principles and causes and is also the "only free science" (982b25ff.): "Acquiring it might be justly regarded, then, as beyond human power; for in many ways human nature is in bondage, so that according to Simonides 'God alone can have this privilege,' but, as the proverb says, "poets tell many a lie," and no science should be thought more worthy [*timiōteran*] than one of this sort; the most worthy science is also the most divine [*theiotatē*]."

11. The word "separate" (*chōristos*), which Aristotle uses to describe the object of first philosophy, does not mean only separable from matter but, as shown at *Metaphysics* 1028a34–35, must be understood first and foremost in relation to language: "None of the other categories," writes Aristotle here, referring back to the treatise on *Categories*, "can be separable [*outhen chōriston*], but only existence [*hē ousia*], which will be first according to language." The primary character of *ousia* is stated forcefully at *Categories* 2b5: "If the primary *ousiai* did not exist, it would be impossible for any of the others to exist; indeed, all the others are said on the sup-position of the latter" (*kath'hupokeimenōn toutōn*). For this reason, the way *ousia prōtē* is treated in the *Categories* (which coincides with the deictic "this certain man, this certain horse") is inseparable from how the same problem is treated in the *Metaphysics*. It is impossible to properly understand first philosophy's status in Aristotle unless one grasps the connection between ontology and language implicit in the thesis that "being *is said* in many ways": even before the

multiplicity of being's saying, it is essential that being be said. Thus, at 1028a10ff., *ousia* is defined from the point of view of language, just as in the treatise on the *Categories*: *ousia* is not what we designate with an accidental predicate such as "good" or "white" (*leukon*) or "three cubits high" (*tripēchu*), but with a noun such as "human" or "god." The object of first philosophy is expressed in language through the same terms in which *ousia* is expressed in the *Categories*, as being different from quantity and quality (the examples here are the same as in the *Metaphysics*: "white, three cubits high"). And it is worth remembering that the doctrine of *ousia* developed in *Categories* is based on an analysis of the meaning of names ("that which is said without connection," *aneu sumplokēs*, such as "man, ox, runs, wins"), that is, an analysis of the lexicon and not of speech in action.

If one can speak of anything like a split of the object of first philosophy in Aristotle's thought, it is not to be found in the duality of *on* and *theos*, metaphysics and theology, but in the fundamental division described in the *Categories* between *ousiai prōtai* and *ousiai deuterai*, between what is not said of a presupposed subject (*hupokeimenon*) and is not in a presup-posed subject and what is said of a presupposed subject and is in a presup-posed subject. The primacy of first philosophy in the *Metaphysics* corresponds exactly to the primacy of prime substances in the *Categories*, just as the being of the *Metaphysics* corresponds to the *ousia* of the proper name or to the deictic of the *Categories*.

12.   That the *Categories* is an analysis of what is said "without connection," of the lexicon and not of speech

in action, is reiterated by Aristotle immediately after he lists the ten categories: "Each of the terms in and of itself [*hekaston de tōn eiremenōn auto men kath'auto*; the translation "each of the things said is said in itself," by introducing the word "thing" unduly, suggests that Aristotle is referring to things and not also, and primarily, to words] is not said in any affirmation [*kataphasei*, discourse about something], since an affirmation is produced only through the reciprocal connection [*tēi sumplokēi*] between such terms. For every affirmation is either true or false, but terms with no connection can be neither true nor false" (2a5–10). In the *Sophist*, Plato had earlier observed in a similar sense that "a succession of names said one after the other does not yet make discourse [*oudeis pō sunestē logos*], nor does it arise from the verbs unless they are accompanied by the names [. . .]. Words do not indicate an action or an inaction or the existence [*ousian*] of a being or a nonbeing, until the names are mingled with the verbs" (262c).

This fundamental division at the level of language corresponds to the distinction in modern linguistics between *langue* and *parole* and between signification and denotation: a term has a meaning at the lexical level (Aristotle calls it *logos tēs ousias*), but it acquires a denotation (a real reference) only in discourse. We do well to remember that ancient Greeks were perfectly aware of these divisions, although (not unlike most moderns in this respect) they did not always draw the consequences that the divisions implied at the level of thought.

13.   In a brilliant essay, Émile Benveniste shows that the Aristotelian categories reproduce the structures of the Greek language and are therefore categories of language

before they are of thought. Thus the first category, *ousia*, corresponds to the class of substantives or nouns,[22] which ancient grammarians called by this name specifically in reference to Aristotle's *ousia*. Crucially, however, Aristotle introduces into the first category the split between *ousiai prōtai* and *ousiai deuterai*, primary and secondary substances, a split that would prove decisive in the history of metaphysics. This split is all the more problematic as it somehow calls into question the division of the linguistic sphere into lexicon and discourse, signification and denotation, on which the *Categories* treatise is founded. *Ousia prōtē*, exemplified in this sense by "this certain man, this certain horse," splits the sphere of nouns (substantives) according to whether they function as the "ultimate subject" (*hupokeimenon*, lying under, as a pre-supposition) in a discourse or are instead predicated of a subject. Primary substances are said to be substances chiefly "because they are pre-supposed in [*hupokeisthai*, they serve as subjects to, or underlie] all the other [categories] and because all these others are predicated of them" (2b15). Thus the primary substance is "the ultimate subject [*hupokeimenon eschaton*] that cannot be predicated of anything else" (*Metaphysics* 1017b23). The primary substances in some way define the threshold between *langue* and *parole* (between nouns and discourse) and between signification and denotation. If a substantive can be inserted into a proposition as an ultimate subject, it is therefore "called *ousia* most properly, primarily, and principally" [*kuriōtata te kai prōtōs kai malista legomenē*] (2a11). Since this threshold is not examined in these terms in the *Categories*, the problem it leaves unresolved can only reappear in the treatment of *ousia* in the *Metaphysics*.

———

It is the primacy of *ousia prōtē* that Aristotle will call into question at *Metaphysics* 1029a9–12, when he writes that the determination of the primary *ousia* in the *Categories* is "inadequate and obscure," and he introduces the *ti einai* in its place. Rudolf Boehm has shown that this new definition of *ousia* introduces a split in being, so that being is divided into an inessential existent (an inaccessible lying-at-the-base) and a comprehensible but inexistent essence. "Essence and existence fall outside each other and in this way break with each other, in both senses of the word: they break with each other and they fall into pieces."[23] The being of the *Categories* thus becomes a past in the *Metaphysics*: "*to ti ēn einai*, what it *was* [*ēn*] [for a certain being] to be." This is easily understood, if we recall that the categories are what is said with no connection, and therefore they correspond to an analysis of nouns, of language as lexicon, whereas what is in question in the *Metaphysics* is language as *logos*, as discourse. For this reason, the question *ti to on* is aporetic and must always be queried anew: if *on hēi on* means "the term 'existent' inasmuch as it denotes an existent in a discourse," the question about *ousia* in itself can only take this form: "what *was* it for that certain subject [*hupokeimenon*] to exist?"

Continuing with Benveniste's analysis, if we ask about the linguistic form that Aristotle chose for his question on being, it certainly does not appear accidental that it involves a participle (*on*, being), that is, an intermediary form between noun and verb, which owes its name to the fact that it partakes in the characters of both. Apollonius Dyscolus, in his *Syntax*, speaks of it as a third part of speech, after the noun and the verb, and defines it as the transformation of the verb into an inflectional form, that is, a noun. It is perhaps owing to the participle's hybrid nature that it does not appear on the list of categories, where the examples of verbal forms are given in the infinitive (to lie, to have, to do), and the first category is represented by a term that is the substantivization of a verbal form: *ousia*, "essence," that is, the fact or action of being (*einai*). Nor is it an accident that, when he tries to define what *ousia* is, Aristotle does not use the participle but the infinitive: *to ti ēn einai*, what it was to be. The question *ti to on*, what is being, is aporetic also because the form in which it is expressed is itself problematic. Inasmuch as *on hēi on* partakes of both noun and verb, it defines a threshold of indifference between meaning and denotation.

14. Essential to understanding the object of first philosophy, therefore, is an examination of the concept of language implicit in it. The difference between the Aristotelian and the Platonic ways of posing the question of being appears here in all its relevance. In the passage cited from the *Seventh Letter*, Plato states that one cannot grasp the real essence (i.e. "the truly existent") unless the first four are grasped, that is, the name, the discourse, the sensible being, and the knowledge. But he is careful to point out immediately that in language it is impossible to separate being from its qualities and properties ("owing to the weakness inherent in language, the first four express the quality [*to poion ti*] of each object no less than its being [*to on*]," 342e). The name is no exception; indeed, Plato specifies that there is no certainty in it and nothing to prevent one name from being mistaken for another. In contrast, Aristotle believes that he possesses a language that, insofar as it "signifies one thing" (*hen sēmainei*), is capable of saying *ousia* immediately. The demonstration by refutation of the most certain of all principles, the principle of noncontradiction, is based precisely on

the fact that, in every discourse, the name can ultimately be traced back to one meaning. "For it is not possible," he writes in Book Γ, "to think of anything if we do not think of one thing [*hen*]; but if this is possible, one name might be assigned to this thing" (1006b10), and the name ultimately means something and something about one thing (*sēmainon ti to onoma kai sēmainon hen*, 1006b13). If the name does indeed signify one thing, then this is the *ousia* of the thing ("there must, then, even in this case be something that signifies the *ousia*," 1007b16). A linguistic fact – the semantic character of the name – serves as the foundation for an ontological theorem.

While Aristotle can thus ask about being qua being, Plato thinks that one cannot ask the question about being without at the same time questioning the language in which that question is asked. In Aristotle's terms, one could say that Plato questions the "as" – the *hēi* – between the two occurrences of *on* (the existent insofar as it is *said to be* existent), which Aristotle, by focusing exclusively on the *on*, leaves unquestioned.

In this sense, Rüdiger Bubner's thesis that "ontology is the doctrine of the construction of that reality that is necessary to fulfill determinate linguistic structures"[24] is certainly correct. However, this idea should also be flipped around: that language is constructed in such a way as to allow reality to be understood. The structure of a determinate historical language not only is a natural given but is itself largely conditioned by philosophical and grammatical reflection, that is, by the process through which speakers become progressively aware of what they are doing when they speak and thereby transform the *factum loquendi* into a language, namely an instrument of knowledge and control over reality. At stake in philosophy, then, is a continuous grappling between thought and language in which neither contender can claim to get to the bottom of the reasons and conditions that each continues to propose to and impose on the other.

15. Book Γ opens with the thesis that "[t]here is a science which studies [*theōrei*, contemplates] being qua being and the affections which belong to it inherently." This science, Aristotle continues, is not identical to the sciences that are called "particular" (*en merēi*): "none of these others deals generally with being qua being, but, having cut off [*apotemomenai*] a part of it, they investigate the accidents of this part, as the mathematical sciences do for instance" (1003a20–26). At issue are the unity and, along with it, the divisions – the cuts or regional sections – of philosophy as a science of being. Indeed, immediately afterwards Aristotle sets out the theorem that, starting with Brentano's book, has become the emblem of his ontology: "being is said in many ways [*to on legetai pollachōs*], but with reference to a unity and to one nature, but not as homonyms [*pros hen kai mian phusin, kai ouch homonumos*]" (1003a33). Aristotle calls "homonyms" things that have the same name but a different definition, and "synonyms" things that have the same name and the same definition. As Alexander of Aphrodisias sensed in his comment, this is a matter of defining the special unity, neither homonymous nor synonymous, that characterizes being: "Having said that there is a science concerned with being qua being and with its principles and its causes, and having established it with the name of wisdom, he [Aristotle] shows how it is possible for there to be a single science of being, even though being is considered a homonym and in homonymous things there cannot be one nature or one art or science or one

and the same principle. That is, he divides the things grouped under a common term into homonymous, synonymous, and, finally, things named according to a unity or by reference to a oneness [*aph'henos tinos ē pros hen ti legomena*]."[25] Alexander suggests that Aristotle conceptualizes being as something in-between homonyms and synonyms, and that between them he inserts those things that he considers "with reference to a unity and to one nature." These include neither the sameness of the predicate that defines synonyms nor the radical heterogeneity proper to homonyms: "rather they have a certain commonality, which consists in the fact that, if they are what their name expresses, they owe it to the existence of a certain nature of the thing that is their principle, to which they all bear a certain relation [*logon*] and because of which they share the same name."[26]

If we recall that Aristotle, in his discussion of Platonic theory, had defined the relationship between sensible things and ideas using the formula "the multitude of synonyms is homonymous through participation in the Ideas" (987b10), what he is after in Book Γ is precisely the status of unity that, beyond homonymy and synonymy, belongs in its own right to the *on hēi on*; and this is what he will call *ousia*. Ricoeur has suggested that the unity in question is that of analogy, but this hardly simplifies the problem, given that, as has been noted authoritatively, "The only interest Aristotle devotes to analogy is distracted, marginal, and, at least in analytical terms, clearly derogatory."[27] Indeed, none of the passing definitions that Aristotle gives of analogy (equality of relations between at least four terms, *Eth. Nic.* 1131b31; as part to part, *An. Pr.* 69a13–16; as a third thing is to a fourth, *Met.* 1016b34) are applicable to being qua being. On the other hand, despite the fact that he seems at times to be speaking of genus and species, Aristotle explicitly excludes the notion that being can constitute a genus (*ou gar genos to on, An. Post.* 92b). The only possible conclusion is that the unity of first philosophy remains problematic from the outset and that its relationship with the "cuts" of the particular sciences cannot be defined unequivocally.

It is possible, then, that what the moderns call analogy, the *pros hen* to which the various meanings of being refer, in reality conceals the problem of the original splitting of *ousia* that metaphysics seeks to resolve. In other words, at issue in the *pros hen* is the pure fact that being is said, within or beyond the *pollachōs*, of the many ways in which it is said. We can therefore define the "one" to which the multiple ways of saying can be traced back as the "being-said," the mere fact of having a name in language. And it is evident that such a being-said (being insofar as it *said* to be being) is neither a meaning nor a denotation; it is not entirely ascribable to *langue* or to *parole*, but it refers to the original status of language within or beyond the split into meaning and denotation. As such, it can never be reached as "one," it has no place of its own, but it arises each time in the multiplicity of its terms (*legomena*).

16. We can now attempt to define with greater precision the issue in what appears to modern scholars as an inconsistency in Aristotle's thought on metaphysics and first philosophy. At issue in this discrepancy is the oneness of philosophical knowledge, a matter that Aristotle poses problematically from the very beginning

of Book Γ. If "it is the work of one science to study beings qua beings" (1003b15), this does not exclude, however, that this science is then articulated into various species (1003b22). And if, in the passage quoted above, it is stated that there are "as many parts [merē] of philosophy as there are substances [ousiai]," in Book E the three "theoretical philosophies" – mathematics, physics, and theology – are structured together according to a complex relationship that includes the primacy of theology and, along with it, the impossibility of defining its object except in relation to the other two. In other words, first philosophy names an epistemic space whose unity is on the one hand openly asserted and on the other incessantly called into question. The strong bond between these two movements allowed Aristotle to write that first philosophy is constituted through differentiation from physics, and therefore that "the concept of first philosophy is a concept of second philosophy."[28] What the western tradition has come to call "metaphysics" is not so much an autonomous discipline as the place where the boundaries between philosophy and the other sciences are decided, in order to ensure the unity of knowledge and at the same time to govern the conflicts that arise from the internal partitions within this purported unity.

If western thought has done nothing "of old, at present, and always" but ask the question "What is being?," and if this question has led it down a dead end, this is perhaps because, as early as in Aristotle's Categories, the object of first philosophy, having been split, is not properly one object. The moment ousia in the Categories fell into a discourse and became "that which it was for that certain determinate being to be" (*to ti ēn einai*), its *ergon* could only be the placement of a plurality of discourses and knowledges, each one defined by a determinate object. In other words, the problem of first philosophy is not so much the purported split between metaphysics and theology as the internal partition of theoretical knowledge into at least three sciences or "philosophies." This is how theoretical knowledge establishes itself as the primary dimension, of which the sciences – especially mathematics and physics – are *merē*, that is, according to the original meaning of the word, regions or parts assigned as "fates" (*moirai*).[29] First philosophy assigned the physical sciences and mathematics to the West as its destiny. At the same time, in the same gesture, in carving out an object from this destination that is every bit as residual as it is problematic, it set itself up as sovereign (*kuriōtatē*, 1064b1) over them.

As Plato noted (*Rep.* 607b), there is an ongoing *palaia diaphora* in western culture, not only between philosophy and poetry but especially between philosophy and science: an old dispute whose inception coincides with the Aristotelian placement of first philosophy. No wonder, then, that the unity of western knowledge, which has been uncertain and threatened from the outset, has arrived at a breaking point, whose full gravity we are only just beginning to fathom. The articulation of theoretical knowledge, which claimed to maintain unity through a tripartite division that ensured philosophy's sovereignty over the other sciences, has proved precarious, perhaps because it pursued at all costs a nonexistent coherence. Indeed, it would certainly have been possible to establish other boundaries, which, by separating their respective spheres more clearly and distinctly and possibly by renouncing the role of science, would have ensured both philosophy and the sciences not sovereignty or dependence, but a full and reciprocal autonomy. Wanting to ensure its primacy over the sciences and at the same time assigning them to the West as its fate, philosophy ended up instead subjugating itself to them without realizing it. And after having long set itself up as the handmaid of theology, *ancilla theologiae*, today it is, in all evidence, just a powerless handmaid to the sciences, *ancilla scientiarum*.

2
Philosophy Divided

1. The word "metaphysics," in its Latin form *meta-physica*, was invented by Domenicus Gundissalinus (aka Domingo Gundisalvo or Gundisalvi, c. 1110–1190), someone whose life we know little about. We do know that he played a unique role in the history of philosophy as a translator from the Arabic of Solomon ibn Gabirol, of al-Fârâbî, and, above all, of the metaphysics section of Avicenna's *Kitâb al-shifâ* (*The Book of Healing*) (he translated the latter under the title *Liber de philoso-phia prima*, in collaboration with a Jewish translator, Avendauth, following the practice of the Toledo school of translators). His activity is all the more pivotal as, until his time, the phrase *ta meta ta phusika* had been used exclusively to designate a work by Aristotle, while the corresponding discipline was commonly referred to as theology. Boethius uses the expression four times in his commentaries, as a bibliographical reference, but when he means the corresponding discipline he uses the expression "theological science" instead. "There are three parts of speculative science," he writes in *De*

trinitate (ch. 2), "one of which, the *natural*, deals with things [. . .] that are not abstract [*inabstracta*], that is, the forms of bodies along with their matter, since the form cannot be separated in reality from their bodies [. . .]. The *mathematical* is concerned with things that are without motion but not abstract [. . .]. The *theological* is concerned with things without motion that are abstract and separable, for the substance of God lacks both matter and motion."[1] Arabic authors, too, use the transliteration *matâtâfusîqâ* or the literal translation "that which is after nature" for the book, and instead call the corresponding subject matter *al-'ilm al-ilâhî*, that is, "the science of divine things."[2] In some of Abelard's manuscripts, the formula *meta ta phusika* is abbreviated to *meta phusika*, but the expression always refers to Aristotle's book.

In Gundissalinus' prologue to his *De divisione philosophiae* (*On the Division of Philosophy*), the word *metaphysica* makes its first appearance discretely, as a synonym of "first philosophy" and, in an unexpected inversion of the Aristotelian order, "third" after physics and mathematics. Gundissalinus begins with a eulogy of the good old days ("Happy was the ancient age, which produced so many wise men, like stars that light up the darkness of the world") and then goes on to explain: "The first part of the division is called physical or natural science, which is the first and the lowest. The second is called mathematics or disciplinary science and is the middle one. The third is called theology, or first science, or first philosophy, or metaphysics" (*tercia dicitur theologia sive sciencia prima sive philosophia prima sive metaphysica*).[3] Earlier on, he explained the names of first philosophy and metaphysics thus: "It is called first philosophy since it is the science of the first cause of being. It is also called the cause of the causes, since it concerns God, who is the cause of everything. It is also called metaphysics, that is, 'after the physics' [*post physicam*], since it concerns that which is after nature [*de eo quod est post naturam*]."[4] This posteriority (*posteritas*) of metaphysics vis-à-vis physics does not pertain to the science itself, but to the order of our cognitive faculty: "considered in itself, this science should rather be called 'before nature' [*ante naturam*], since that which it investigates essentially as science is before nature."[5]

2.   The definition of first philosophy as a science about God (*quia in ea agitur de Deo*) seems to contradict what Gundissalinus had written a little earlier, when he explained that the subject matter of this science is not God but "that which is more general and obvious [*communius et evidentius*] than everything else, namely being [*ens*]."[6] This contradiction is at least partly resolved if we keep in mind that the first definition was contained in his explanation of the name of metaphysics (*quare sic vocatur*), whereas the second refers to its subject matter. Repeating one of Avicenna's theses, Gundissalinus affirms here that those who posited God as the subject matter of metaphysics were deceived because, "according to Aristotle's testimony, no science can investigate [the existence of] its own subject matter, whereas this science explores whether God exists. Therefore, God is not its subject matter."[7] The contradiction does not disappear, however, because, on the matter of the genus it should be assigned to, Gundissalinus affirms unreservedly that, insofar as it deals with that which is separate from matter and motion, it "concerns the cause of

causes and the principle of principles, which is God."[8] It has been suggested that he was probably trying to come to terms with an aporia already present in Aristotle's work that states several times that being is not a genus; and yet he seems to imply nonetheless that every science has a presupposed genus (*genos hupokeimenon*) (*An. Post.* 75a42). Also, at *Metaphysics* 1026a21, Aristotle defines the object of first philosophy as the "most honorable genus" (*timiōtaton genos*). Once again, the split in first philosophy's object is not so much between being and the divine as it is between the various meanings of the word *on* and the *pros hen*: the unity to which they refer by analogy. If, according to *Metaphysics* 1016b34, the unity between elements that do not belong to the same genus can be called analogical, this in no way defines this unity.

3. We do well to reflect on the title of the book, which takes for granted that philosophy is constitutively divided into parts. The incipit of the manuscript is decidedly eloquent about the essentiality of this partition: "The book begins with the division of philosophy into its parts and the parts into their parts according to the philosophers" (*Incipit liber de divisione philosophie in partes suas et parcium in partes suas secundum philosophos*). And the idea that this division at the same time implies the hierarchical primacy of philosophy is stated forcefully in the theorem "there is no science that is not a part of philosophy" (*nulla est sciencia que philosophie non sita aliqua pars*):[9] philosophy is constitutively compartmentalized, and this partitioning includes not only physics and mathematics but all the sciences to some extent. All disciplines are part of the first (or last)

---

knowledge, whose province is "all that enlightens the human soul with the knowledge of the truth and fires it with love of good."[10] This is why *On the Division of Philosophy* includes all the arts and sciences in its analysis, from grammar to medicine and astronomy to music: although not technically parts of the science of being, they all come "under the science that deals with being" (*sub sciencia, que tractat de ente*).[11]

The primacy of metaphysics over the other sciences is based on its capacity to validate their principles. "Since the principles of the sciences are not self-evident, it is necessary that they be examined in other sciences, either in a science as particular as this science or in a science which is more common. In that case one would finally reach a science that is more common than all the others. Therefore, the principles of the other sciences must be verified [*certificientur*] by this science [. . .]. First philosophy is more common than all the particular sciences because of the commonality of its subject."[12]

The moment Aristotle's first philosophy receives the name from which it will be separated nevermore, having become metaphysics, it continues to be defined by an internal split and, simultaneously, by its unconditional pretense of sovereignty over the other sciences.

4.   The translation of Avicenna's and Averroes' works into Latin coincides with the division of first philosophy into two camps, depending on whether its object is *ens*, as Avicenna asserts, or God and the separate intelligences, as Averroes maintains. The opposition between ontology and theology that the moderns have projected onto Aristotle's text seems here to take its most radical formulation. We need only examine the arguments

of the individual authors, however, to see that they are by no means a peremptory alternative between two mutually exclusive terms. Thomas Aquinas, like his teacher Albert the Great, belongs in the ranks of those who assert, in agreement with Avicenna, that the *subiectum* of metaphysics is being qua being, and not God. Nevertheless, if we read Aquinas' commentary on Boethius' *On the Trinity*, we discover that not only is God not excluded from metaphysics, but knowledge of God actually constitutes its proper end. For every science must presuppose its subject as a given to which all the objects can be traced, either through a deduction from a known cause to unknown effects (*propter quid*) or through a deduction from known effects to an unknown cause (*propter quia*). But, since our intellect relates to divine things as the eye of an owl relates to the light of the sun (*ut oculus noctuae ad lucem solis*), we can attain knowledge of them only the second way. This is why philosophers cannot concern themselves with divine things as the subject of their science, but only insofar as they are the unknown principle of the beings with which the science of being qua being is concerned. For this reason, the divine science is twofold: a science "that treats of divine things, not as the subject of the science but as the principles of the subject. This is the kind of theology pursued by the philosophers and that is also called metaphysics. The other science investigates divine things for their own sake as the subject of the science. This is the theology taught in Sacred Scripture" (*In Boethii De trinitate*, V, 4).

John of Paris, aka Quidort ("the Sleeper," Fr. *qui dort*), an undoubtedly original writer who risked condemnation for challenging the doctrine of transubstantiation,

---

begins by distinguishing between the subject (*subiectum*) and the matter (*materia*) of a science: "One can call the matter of a science everything that is dealt with and defined in it, while one calls the subject only that which is assumed to be already known to it."[13] Therefore God cannot be the object of metaphysics, because metaphysics cannot presuppose Him as known, but seeks to know Him from His creatures. He can be conceptualized, however, as a part of its subject, that is, of a being. Quidort concludes boldly that "the subject of metaphysics is therefore superior to the subject of theology," although he is compelled out of caution to add that, "despite this, theology is not subordinate to metaphysics."[14]

The wording John Duns Scotus uses to formulate the problem of metaphysics' twofold object is crucial. He begins by recalling the opposing positions of Avicenna and Averroes and concludes, *neutrum probo*, "I agree with neither." The reasons for his "neutrality" are so complex that, after investigating to what extent it would be possible to regard God as the subject of metaphysics, as Averroes would have it, Duns Scotus seems to affirm, along with Avicenna, that the subject cannot be God, but only being qua being.

Like Aquinas, he affirms that the subject of a science can be the object of a knowledge *propter quid* or *propter quia*, that is, a science that proceeds from the effects to the cause. A deduction *propter quid* with respect to God is impossible, for the human intellect cannot know God through a cause that would be anterior to Him. ("Such an imperfect metaphysics the angels could possess, perhaps, if they were pilgrims [i.e. in the earthly condition] for a long time."[15]) The only possible knowledge is *propter quia*, and it is according to this second paradigm that Duns Scotus considers again the possibility, in opposition to Avicenna, that God is the subject of metaphysics. But in this case too, working back from beings to God, the knowledge of beings as such is necessarily prior to the knowledge that traces them back to God. The metaphysics that has God as its subject must be preceded by "another metaphysics" (*alia metaphysica*), which would be concerned with beings qua beings. Metaphysics can present itself as the science of being qua being only on condition that it presupposes and at the same time transcends the other sciences, which now become three: in addition to mathematics and physics, there is also theology (namely the metaphysics whose subject is God). First philosophy thus becomes constitutively *scientia trascendens* – in the sense that its object, as we shall see, is the transcendental predicates, and because it is defined constitutively by its transcending the other special sciences: "Thus, transcendent metaphysics is wholly prior to the divine science, and there will be four theoretical sciences, one transcendent and three special sciences" (*Ita metaphysica transcendens est tota prior scientia divina, et ita essent quatuor scientiae speculativae, una transcendens et tres speciales*).[16] Once again, metaphysics is always defined in relation to other "special" disciplines, which it transcends and presupposes at the same time.

3
Critique of the Transcendental

Metaphysicus est artifex universalis et trascendens atque primus philosophus per se passiones entis in quantum ens inquirens.

The Metaphysician is the universal artificer, the transcendent, the first philosopher, who by himself investigates the affections of Being in so far as it is Being.

Nicholas Bonet, *Metaphysica*,
translation by Bertrand Russell

1.   Beginning in the fourteenth century, the concept of metaphysics was transformed, changing the history of western thought in ways we have yet to fully gauge. This transformation, coinciding with the invention of the transcendentals – especially the emergence of the transcendental (or supertranscendental) *res* – shifted the object of first philosophy from the existent to representation, from the sphere of being to that of knowledge (or, as Henry of Ghent and others after him would say, from *obiectum*, the real object, to *obiectivum*, the pure

correlate of every act of cognition, independently of its existence outside the mind). The relationship between metaphysics and the other sciences, which I have sought to reconstruct here in Aristotle's work, also changed as a consequence. If metaphysics no longer delimits a field of being, the broadest and most common, each of whose regions is assigned to a science, but instead demarcates a sphere of knowledge, namely the most generic and indeterminate one, then the autonomy of the disciplines that replace this objectless knowledge with effective operations and determinate content consolidates itself even more.

The first treatment of transcendentals, which was to have such an enduring lineage in the history of philosophy up until Kant and beyond, is usually found in Philip the Chancellor's *Summa de bono* (ca. 1230). In reality, the word *transcendens*, which medieval philosophers used all the time, does not appear in the text. But in the Prologue, just after stating what the treatise is about (*de bono autem intendimus, principaliter quod ad theologiam pertinet*, "but we concern ourselves with the good mainly because it belongs to theology," Philip mentions the future transcendentals in the order that will remain unchanged: "the most common [*communissima*] [terms] *are* the following: being, one, true, and good [*ens, unum, verum, bonum*]."[1] Soon afterward unity, truth, and goodness are defined as "the three concomitant conditions of being. The first of these is unity, the second is truth, the third is goodness" (*dicendum quod sunt tres conditiones concomitantes esse: unitas, veritas, bonitas*). The fact is, continues the author, that "every essence has three conditions that accompany its being insofar as it exists, starting from the first being" *(quae concomitantur esse eius secundum quod est a primo ente).*[2]

Philip is a compiler rather than an original thinker. The notions he uses to characterize his "conditions" – commonality and concomitance – derive from Avicenna's *Metaphysics* (in the latter, *ens*, *res*, and *aliquis* are defined as "common to all things," *communia ... omnibus rebus*, and "concomitant," *comitantia*). We will return to their fundamental importance for the development of the scholastic doctrine of the transcendentals. But it is essential that both characteristics that will define the transcendentals be present: they must be the most general terms, common to all things; and they must be inseparable from being to the point of almost coinciding with it. Scholasticism would specify that these terms are called "transcendent" because they transcend each of Aristotle's categories, and the technical term to define their mutual relationship would no longer be concomitance but convertibility: *ens*, *unum*, *verum*, and *bonum* can be converted into one another (*convertuntur*). When we say *ens*, when we say that something is, we also mean that it is one, true, and good, just as saying one, true, and good means at the same time referring to an existent.

The first occurrence of the term *trascendentia* is in the commentary on Aristotle's *Peri hermeneias* (*On Interpretation*) written by Johannes Pagus (John Le Page) between 1231 and 1235, which mentions "something and one, thing and being" (*aliquid et unum, res et ens*) as transcendental names (*nomina trascendentia*), and in Roland of Cremona's *Summa theologica* (c. 1244), where they appear in the order *ens*, *unum*, *aliquid*, and *res*.[3] In both cases, the list adds "thing" and "something" to the two terms that feature in Philip the Chancellor's work (*ens* and *unum*). But already in Thomas Aquinas *res* and *aliquid* are added to the four terms recorded by Philip (*ens, unum, verum, bonum*). Chapter 2 of the treatise *De natura generis* (traditionally attributed to Aquinas) begins with the words: *Sunt autem sex transcendentia, videlicet ens, res, aliquid, unum, verum, bonum: quae re idem sunt, sed ratione distinguuntur* ("There are six transcendentals, namely being, thing, something, one, true, and good: which are essentially the same but are distinguished by reason").

When defining the term *trascendens* (exemplified by *ens, res, unum, aliquid, verum,* and *bonum*), the fourteenth-century lexicon titled significantly *Declaratio difficilium terminorum (Clarification of Difficult Terms)* states that it is "one of those names that express the mode of being inherent in a general way in all beings," and adds that "transcendent signifies so to speak beyond each being [*quasi trans omne ens*] or also passing beyond every being [*transiens omne ens*]."[4] This can be understood as referring to existence, and so one says transcendent God, "because He transcends all beings by the nobility of actual existence." But the lexicon is careful to point out that this is not the way the term is commonly used, since it refers rather to the common character of the predication (*a praedicationis communitate*) and designates "that which one can predicate of all beings." It has been suggested that the transcendence in question here is a "semantic transcendence," because it is situated at the level of signification, which pushes toward its furthest limit and greater generality – with the proviso, however, that here "semantic" should be understood starting from the split between meaning and denotation. Both the opposition between the two senses of the term *trascendens* in the *Declaratio* and, more generally, that between being qua being and God as the object of first philosophy can be traced back to this split.

2. The foundation for the medieval doctrine of transcendentals lies in Aristotle. In *Metaphysics*, just before the demonstration by refutation of the principle of non-contradiction, we read (1003b22ff.) that "being [*to on*] and the one [*to hen*] are identical and have one

nature, because of their following upon one another [*akolouthein allēlois* – this is the verb that the scholastics would translate as *converti*] [. . .] For *one* human [*heis anthrōpos*] and a human or an existing human [*on anthrōpos*] and a human are the same thing, and nothing else is made clear by the doubling of the expression 'he is a human' and 'he is an existing human.'" In Book K (1061a15–17) Aristotle adds that "it makes no difference whether the reference [*anagōgēn*, "bringing back," which medieval authors would translate as *reductio*] to that which is is to being or to the one [*pros to on ē pros to hen gignesthai*], for even if [the terms] are not the same, in actuality somehow the one reverses [*antistrephei*, literally turns the opposite way – medieval authors would translate this as *converti*] into being and being is one [*to te on ēn*]." And in *Nicomachean Ethics* (1096a24), speaking also of the good (*agathon*), he writes that "things are said to be good in as many ways as they are said to be" (*isachōs legetai tōi onti*).

It has been aptly observed[5] that this does not mean that there is a systematic doctrine of transcendentals in Aristotle and that no Aristotelian text allows the one and the good to be placed on the same plane of being as the object of first philosophy. No less pertinently, it has been noted, however, that "Aristotle's concept of *akolouthein* ['to follow'] and, even more, that of *antistrephein* ['to convert'] rather clearly open the way to the scholastic notion of convertibility."[6]

3. The entrance of the "thing" into first philosophy and into what would become the doctrine of transcendentals had a pivotal place in Avicenna. In a passage from *Metaphysics* that would garner constant attention

from medieval philosophers, he states that "thing" (*res*; *shay* in Arabic) and "being" (*ens*) are original and immediately knowable (in the Latin translation, *statim imprimuntur in anima prima impressione*, "instantly leave their first stamp on the soul"), common to all things (*communia* [. . .] *omnibus rebus*) and not derivable from other, better known notions (*quae non acquiritur ex aliis notioribus se*) and therefore not definable except in a circular way (*nullo modo potest manifestari aliquid horum probatione quae non sit circularis*). "How in fact," he asks ironically, "can 'the thing' be known, since only through it can everything be known?"[7]

Although the two concepts "being" and "thing" [*cosa*] are extensionally identical, they differ intentionally, namely according to the mode of meaning: while "being" concerns things insofar as they are beings, *cosa* refers rather to their essence. "Every thing," writes Avicenna, "has an essence [Arabic: *haqiqa*; Latin: *certitudo*] through which it is what it is, just as the triangle has an essence that defines it as a triangle and whiteness an essence that defines it as such."[8] From *shay* he forges the word *shay'iyya*, "cosality," which, owing to a miscommunication between Dominic Gundissalinus and Avendauth, whom he was translating orally from Arabic into Spanish, was rendered into Latin as *causalitas* instead of *realitas* or the neologism "cosalitas." In Avicenna's thought, then, partly perhaps because of this translation error, "thing" is an ambiguous term, designating on the one hand the primordial impression from which all cognition arises and, on the other, the essence or what Latin authors would call *quidditas* (the "what thing it is" [*il "che cos'è"*]), almost as if the "thing" preceded the distinction between essence and existence while at the same time being somehow a part of it. Indeed, Avicenna realizes that the "thing" is not only that which "first impresses itself on the soul" but also that which underlies every true statement (in the Latin translation, *res est res* – and note the inevitable tautology: the thing is the thing – *de qua vere potest aliquid enuntiari*, "that about which something can truly be said"[9]). In this sense, it is presupposed and always already included not only in every statement but also in every definition – necessarily circular – that one may wish to give it. And yet, although Avicenna distinguishes it in this sense from being, he can state that the thing is inseparable from existence, "because intelligence of being accompanies it constantly."[10]

As Gilson suggested, what Avicenna intends to affirm "is the existence of a transcendental, that is, of a universal more universal than the categories."[11] At this point we may conjecture that, in a culture that cannot yet thematize the problem of language itself, *res*, "thing," names the pure intentionality of language, in other words the fact that every statement refers to something, independently of its factual existence, or somehow before the distinction between existence in the mind and existence in reality ("the thing, writes Avicenna, "can have being in the intellect and not in the external reality," *potest res habere esse in intellectu et non in exterioribus*[12]). Consider the quoted passage in which Avicenna defines essence (*haqiqa*): "every thing [*unaquaeque res*] has an essence through which it is what it is" (p. 43 in this chapter). Here, by all evidence, the "thing" is presupposed by the essence that defines it, but this is not because it designates the object of a perception but because, even before the distinction between essence and existence, it names the intentional correlate of language. It is significant in this sense that, later, the scholastics would use expressions such as *existentia rei* and *essentia rei* without asking themselves about the status of being that *res* holds in them, since both essence and existence refer to it – to *res*.

Once again, Avicenna is to some extent aware of this ambiguity when, in conclusion to the passage cited, he writes: "You have now understood, then, in what way that which is understood by being [*esse*] and that which is understood by something [*aliquid*] differ, even though these two notions are concomitant [*comitantia*]. I have been told that some people say that something is something, even if it has no existence, and that 'something' is the form of a thing, that it is not a thing, and that it neither is nor is not, and that it signifies other than what 'cosa' [*res*] signifies. However, they are not among those who understand."[13] By all evidence, Avicenna seeks here to affirm the difference between thing and being and at the same time to rule out the thing being reduced, as the *kalam mu'tazilita* taught, to something inexistent or to the pure general object of knowledge.

It has been rightly observed[14] that, contrary to the interpretation that would prevail among medieval and modern interpreters, the distinction between "being" and "thing" does not correspond in Avicenna to the difference between existence and essence but to the difference between that which is the object of a discourse (*de qua vere potest aliquid enuntiari*) and that which is affirmed to exist. If my hypothesis is correct, the fact is that, constitutively inherent in what the "thing"

---

designates (that is, in the very intentionality of language, the correlate of each name and each intellection), there is a uniduality anterior to that distinction between essence and existence that, for centuries, the philosophical tradition insisted on drawing from. Being is always already divided: this original split is what philosophy seeks to resolve.

At the beginning of *De ente et essentia* (*On Being and Essence*), Thomas Aquinas identifies an inherent duplicity in the very meaning of the term *ens*. *Ens* is actually said in two different ways (*ens per se dicitur dupliciter*), the first of which refers to reality, the second to language: "In the first way," he writes, *ens* presupposes an existence in reality (*primo modo non potest dici ens, nisi quod aliquid in re ponit*); "in the second, however, *ens* is said of anything about which one can form an affirmative proposition" (*potest dici ens omne illud de quo affirmativa propositio formari potest*). Aquinas specifies, however, that – summarizing – the term "essence" is only said in the first way, that is, with reference to an existing substance (*sumitur essentia ab ente primo modo dicto. Unde Commentator in eodem loco dicit quod ens primo modo dictum est quod significat substantiam rei*).

4. Aquinas' interpretation of the difference in Avicenna between being and thing, in terms of the ontological difference between existence and essence, is evident in the passage of *De veritate* (q. I, art. 1), where he develops the doctrine of the transcendentals. "We can, however, find nothing that can be predicated of every being affirmatively and, at the same time, absolutely, with the exception of its essence by which the being is said to be. To express this, the term *res* is used, which, according to Avicenna at the beginning of the *Metaphysics*, differs from being insofar as being gets its name from the act of being [*ens sumitur ab actu essendi*], whereas

the name *res* expresses the essence or quiddity of the being [*nomen rei exprimit quidditatem vel essentiam entis*]." As for the term "one," Aquinas continues, it expresses the negation that is inherent in every being considered absolutely, that is, its undividedness: "and this is expressed by the name 'one'. For 'one' is simply undivided being." If we then consider being insofar as it is divided from others, "this distinctness is expressed by the word 'something' [*aliquid*], which implies, as it were, some other *quid* [*dicitur enim aliquid quasi aliud quid*]. For, just as a being is said to be 'one' insofar as it is without division in itself, so it is said to be 'something' insofar as it is divided from others."

In his *Commentary on the Sentences* (*Scriptum super IV libros Sententiarum*, II, d. 37, q. I, art. 1), playing on the two meanings of the verb *reor* (to ascertain and to think), Aquinas distinguishes between two different senses of the very notion of "thing," understood as essence. The first refers to a being as a thing existing in nature; the second refers only to its knowability, as something that can be an object of knowledge, independently of its existence in nature. "Thing simply means that which has an ascertained and confirmed existence in nature [*quod habet esse ratum et firmum in natura*]; and it is said in this way, using the name 'thing' in the sense of a certain quiddity or essence [. . .] as Avicenna does by distinguishing between the meaning of being and thing. But because the thing is knowable by its essence, the term 'thing' has been transposed to mean everything that can fall into knowledge or the intellect [*omne id quod in cognitione vel intellectu cadere potest*], in the sense in which *res* derives from *reor, reris* [I think, you think]. This is what things of reason with no ascertained existence in nature [*quae in natura ratum esse non habent*] are called." The distinction between essence and existence, at issue in the word "thing," is stated even more clearly in Book 1 (1, d. 25, q. 1, art. 4). Thing differs from being, because within it reside ambiguously two meanings: the thing insofar as it is thought and the thing insofar as it exists: "Since quiddity can consist in a singular that exists outside the soul as well as in the soul insofar as it is understood by the intellect, for this reason the term 'thing' refers to both – to what is in the soul, in the sense in which it is derived from *reor, reris*, as well as to what exists outside it, in the sense in which *res* is said to be something ratified and confirmed in nature."

A similar distinction between logico-semantic and ontological aspects is found in Aquinas' commentary on Boethius' *On the Hebdomads*. Boethius' axiom states that "being is different from that which is [*id quod est*], indeed, being itself is not yet [*nondum est*], but that which is, having received the form of being [*accepta forma essendi*], is and subsists." Aquinas interprets this first formulation of being's split in the sense that it should not relate "to things, about which he is not yet speaking, but to the definitions and intentions themselves," as if it were simply a question of the meaning of the words: "We mean differently when we say 'being' and when we say 'that which is,' just as we mean one thing when we say 'to run' [*currere*] and another when we say 'he who is running' [*currens*]. Running and being signify abstractly, as whiteness does; but that which is, i.e., being and he who is running, signify concretely, like white" (*Expositio in librum Boethii De hebdomadibus, lect.* 22). Once again, at issue is the distinction between the level of names and meaning and the level of discourse and denotation.

The distinction between the two meanings of *res* is found in almost the same terms in Bonaventura's book on the *Sentences*:[15] "The term *res* in general is said to derive from *reor reris*, and it thus encompasses all that falls into knowledge [*omne illud quod cadit in cognitione*], whether it exist externally or only in opinion. But in its proper sense *res* is termed *ratus, rata, ratum*, from 'that which is confirmed and ratified'; as we apply *ratum* to that which exists not only within knowledge but in the nature of real things [*in rerum natura*]."

5. The process outlined here in the anodyne form of an etymological play on the two meanings of the verb *reor* ("I think" and "I certify") would gradually cause the object of first philosophy to shift more or less consciously from the sphere of being to the realm of knowledge and language. A crucial role in this process would be played by the term "thing," which acquires a kind of primacy among the transcendentals, until it establishes itself, in the sixteenth century, as something of a "supertranscendental."[16] This process was not always conscious, and the ambiguity of the term, suspended as it were between being and knowledge, would never be completely resolved. But it is significant that the opposition between the two meanings of *res* leads back to the two meanings of a verb (*reor*) that belongs wholly to the sphere of reasoning and judging and from which derives the word that translates the Greek *logos* into Latin: *ratio*. If, starting with Aristotle, being is something that is said in many ways (*to on legetai pollachōs*), then it is hardly a matter of indifference whether we stress being or saying, whether the emphasis falls on the

first or the second part of the word "onto-logy." In any case, the thing's primacy as an object of metaphysics – a metaphysics converted into a transcendental science – coincides to such an extent with an eclipse of being that there has been mention of *res* "dethroning the concept of being."[17] The question "sought of old, at present, and always" – *ti to on*, "what is being?" – was transformed into "what is the thing?"

6.   A crucial step in defining the "thing" as the object of metaphysics was taken by Henry of Ghent. As a pure object of thought and a "most common" term, *res* is determined first of all by the fact that it has no contrary except pure nothingness (*purum nihil*): "It must be known that the thing or the something [*res sive aliquid*; Henry will coin for it the technical term *aliquitas*, 'somethingness'] is the most common of them all, which everything contains in a certain similar sphere, considered in such a way that it has no opposite except pure nothingness, which is not nor can it be in a thing outside the intellect nor even in the concept of some intellect, since nothing can move the intellect unless it has some reality."[18]

It has been remarked[19] that Henry distinguishes between two statuses of "thing": one cognitive and the other ontological. Therefore the word designates "the content of any representation, abstracting from its *extra intellectum* reality but not from reality understood as the substance proper to the *cogitable* and the intellect."[20] But Henry takes a further step, in which "thing" seems to refer more to language than to thought. In his *Summa*, he specifies the primary meaning of this most common among transcendentals, defining "thing" not as a cognition in the strict sense but as a "bare precognition" (*praecognitio nuda*), a kind of confused intuition of what is signified by a name: "Precognition is a simple, bare cognition, a confused intellection, which determines nothing in the meaning of the name, not whether it is a being in nature or a nonbeing but only the fact that there is some concept of it, so that *res* is not from *ratitudo* [*a ratitudine*] here but from *reor reris* [. . .]. Therefore knowledge, in the sense of a precognition of what something is, must be understood here only as the fact that something is said through a name [*solum quod dicitur per nomen intelligere oportet*] [. . .] and this is what one learns first through a word [*primum quod per vocem apprehenditur*], and it precedes all other information and knowledge about anything."[21] Even before designating a pure thinkable (*cogitabile*), *res* designates here a simple sayable qua sayable; but the sayability in question pertains to a name qua name – to the meaning that a lexical term has independently of its denotation.

Henry introduces the notion of *aliquitas* ("somethingness") in *Questioni quodlibetali*, in relation to Boethius' distinction between *esse* and *id quod est*. While God is nothing but pure being, the being of creatures is composed of being and something else (*aliquid*) to which being belongs (*creaturae essentia quod non tantum nominat esse, sed etiam aliud cui convenit esse*). The part of the compound that does not correspond to being, Henry calls "somethingness" (*aliquitas*): *creatura continet esse et aliquitatem*. He can thus conclude that "this is how we must understand Boethius' maxim *diversum est esse et id quod est* (being and that which is are different).[22]

7. The medieval theory of transcendentals achieves full expression in the work of John Duns Scotus (1266–1308). Being and the other transcendentals are

predicated univocally of both God and creatures, and "this fundamental unity of the concept 'being' ensures the unity and scientificity of metaphysics"[23] as well as that of *metaphysica specialis*, which for Duns Scotus is theology. Given that the transcendentals are the most knowable things (*maxime scibilia*) and form the object of metaphysics, metaphysics is itself a *scientia transcendens*: "What is most knowable is the most common, and such is being qua being and the others that follow being qua being [. . .]. The fact that the most common things [*communissima*] are known first, as demonstrated by Avicenna, implies that other, more particular things [*specialiora*] cannot be known unless the common ones are known first. Since the knowledge of these *communissima* cannot be conveyed in a particular science, there must exist a universal science that considers these transcendentals in themselves. This science we call metaphysics, which is called thus from *meta*, meaning "beyond," and *ycos*, meaning "science," a quasi transcendent science, since it deals with transcendentals [*quasi transcendens scientia, quia est de trascendentibus*]."[24] As has been observed, the first object of philosophy is not to be understood here as a "first being," whether it be God or substance, but as that which is first in the order of our knowledge (*maxime scibile*).[25]

On the other hand, Duns Scotus criticizes Henry of Ghent's theory on *res sive aliquid* as the most common term – the simple indeterminate object of knowledge. As a purely opinable reality, such a "somethingness" is in itself a pure nothingness. And if one makes it the foundation of transcendentals, these will end up being founded on a nothingness: "I therefore ask what he means by somethingness [*Quaero tunc, quid intelligat per aliquitatem*]. If it involves an opinable reality, since it is just as common to something as it is to nothing, then it will in fact be nothing. And if the *res* as *ratitudo* is founded on somethingness conceived in this fashion, it will be founded on nothingness [*fundatur in nihilo*]."[26] Although Duns Scotus makes metaphysics the science of transcendentals, in keeping with an ambiguity that will always accompany their definition, he never abandons a conception of the thing as actually existing. *Res a reor* always maintains an ambiguous relationship with *res rata*.

8. Once Duns Scotus has defined metaphysics as a transcendental science, he very lucidly questions the relationship between it and the other sciences. Inasmuch as he affirms that it is first in relation to them in terms of clarity of knowledge (*in ordine sciendi distincte*), he admits that it is intended as last in the order of teaching (*in ordine doctrinae*): "Metaphysics according to Avicenna is first according to the order of distinct knowledge, since it must verify the principles of the other sciences [. . .] but Avicenna does not contradict himself when he places it last in the order of teaching and first in distinct knowledge, since [. . .] the principles of the other sciences are known by themselves from the confused conception of their terms [*ex conceptu terminorum confuso*]."[27] Thus, in order to practice his science, "the geometer, as a geometer," does not need principles that are known in themselves, "except for those that are immediately evident through a confused knowledge, which is produced from sensible things, such as 'a line is a length, etc.'" It is up to the "metaphysical geometer," that is, the philosopher who sets

out to study geometry, to "seek the quiddity of those confused terms." The relationship between metaphysics and the sciences is thus caught in a circle of sorts: what purports to be first in relation to the particular sciences in reality follows them: "Once geometry and the other special sciences are known, metaphysics follows with regard to the common concepts, from which it can find its way back, through division, to the search for the quiddity of the terms from the special sciences that it has known."[28] "It is thus clear," concludes Duns Scotus, "in what sense metaphysics is first, and in what sense it is not first" (*quomodo metaphysica est prima et quomodo non est prima*).[29] The precariousness of first philosophy's primacy over the second sciences is particularly apparent here: if the purpose of metaphysics is to verify the principles of the other sciences and if, to do this, the metaphysician must make himself each time a geometer, then metaphysics cannot be truly first. And the fact that the sciences do not really need a metaphysical validation becomes increasingly clear as their growing complexity makes the figure of the "metaphysical geometer" obsolete.

9. Being's slippage toward "thing" (*res a reor reris* and not *a ratum*) is evident in Jean Buridan (c. 1295–1358). As the subject of metaphysics, *ens* is first and foremost a term (*Iste terminus "ens" est subiectum proprium ipsius metaphysicae*[30]). Consequently, Buridan painstakingly analyzes the expression *ens in quantum ens* (being insofar as it is being, being qua being) from the point of view of language. His analysis, as has been observed, immediately assumes a metalinguistic stance.[31] Duns Scotus, whose works he shows he had read carefully,

had previously argued that *in quantum* should not be understood in a reduplicative sense (*non intelligitur ly "in quantum" reduplicative*), that is, causative in a universal sense, "as if one were to say that humans insofar as they are human are rational," which implies that all humans are rational. *In quantum* must be understood rather in a *specificative* sense, given that it specifies the reason why the predicate inheres in the first term – as in the expression "matter, insofar as it is potency, moves toward form."

Buridan takes up Duns Scotus' argument almost verbatim, but moves it decisively to the level of language: decisively, in that he specifies that the term *ens* as the subject of metaphysics is to be understood in its material denotation (*ita quod esset suppositio materialis*), in other words according to the terminology of medieval logicians, since it refers to the word itself and not to a thing *extra animam*, outside the mind – unlike what occurs in a *suppositio personalis*. Therefore it must not be understood in a reduplicative way, which would make the false implication that all beings are the object of metaphysics, but rather "in a specific or determinative sense, that is, to express the reason why this term *ens* is posited as the subject specifically of this science [*ad exprimendum rationem secundum qua iste terminus 'ens' ponitur subiectum proprium huius scientiae*]."[32]

Immediately afterwards, Buridan will reveal what this reason is: it is a matter of understanding *ens* not in the sense of a verbal participle, which by its very nature refers only to the present, but in a nominal sense, that is, as a synonym of "thing" or "something" (*nominaliter, tunc est nomen synonymum cum isto termino "res" vel cum isto termino "aliquid"*), "and it is in this sense that it can be the object of metaphysics" (*et sic est ponendum subiectum in ista scientia*). The nexus between semantics and metaphysics, between the analysis of language and the articulation of being, is particularly evident here, even if not addressed explicitly.

10. As metaphysics gradually becomes identified with a science of transcendentals, and the sphere of the transcendentals is defined from *res* and *aliquid* ("thing" and "something"), the very nature of first philosophy is progressively transformed. As the primary object of this science, *on hēi on* (being qua being) is no longer effectively present, as it certainly was in Aristotle and perhaps still was, at least in part, in Thomas Aquinas. Rather, *on hēi on* becomes the objective correlate of a representation, something that corresponds to the wholly indeterminate meaning of the undefined name "thing." In other words, the transcendentalization of being coincides with the doctrine of being's foundation as ontology. When the word "ontology" makes its appearance in seventeenth-century philosophical vocabulary, the being qua being that forms the object of this science is not that which exists in reality, but *esse obiectivum*, that is, in scholastic terminology, its being the object of a representation in the intellect. Thus in Johannes Clauberg's *Elementa philosophiae sive Ontosophia* (1647), one of the first works in which the word appears, the object of first philosophy is divided into three orders: *Intelligible* (the Intelligible), which has an *esse objectivum* (objective being) only in the intellect; *Aliquid* (Something), to which belong both *esse objectivum*, being in a representation, and *esse reale* (real being), existence; and *Ens reale*, to which both *esse objectivum* and *esse reale*

belong, but as a substratum of the attributes (*in prima philosophia tria sibi gradatim succedunt: Intelligibile, quod habet tantum esse objectivum; Aliquid, quod esse objectivum et esse reale; Ens reale, quod esse objectivum, esse reale et attributa re alia obtinet*).[33]

That the supertranscendental "intelligible" is simply the correlate of a representation, first linguistic and then mental, is evident in Clauberg's definition: "The intelligible is anything, however it may be, that can be thought or said [*quicquid quovis modo est, cogitari ac dici potest*]. Thus I *say* Nothing and while I say it I *think*, and while I think, it *is* in my intellect [*Ita* dico *Nihil, et dum* dico cogito, *et dum* cogito, *est illud in intellecto meo*]."[34]

Perhaps nowhere has the meaning of the Cartesian *cogito* been so clearly defined in its unshakeable connection to language and, simultaneously, to medieval scholasticism's transcendentalization of being. Once again, according to the tradition of the medieval *transcendentia*, the object of metaphysics is the most common predicates, which apply equally to God and creatures; but these highly universal predicates exist only in our intellect: "Beyond the name, God and creatures have something in common, which belongs to the higher and prior [*priorem*] science called first philosophy, or, according to the title of Aristotle's books, Metaphysics. Although there is nothing higher than God, there is nonetheless something so common in our intellect such as to somehow comprehend both God and all other things."[35]

11.   This has led to the observation that "modern metaphysics is not an ontology at all, but rather a tino-logy, a

general science of the *cogitable*, of the thing in the sense of 'something,'"[36] of the *ti* devoid of being that Plato had warned against in *Sophist* (237d); and that, "by concentrating on the *res*, metaphysics attains the status of a science only by abandoning its first object: being."[37] In a clear "reversal of the Platonic–Aristotelian principle by which the more knowable a thing is, the more ontological reality it carries,"[38] the substantiality of *on* is replaced by the simple correlation – eventually devoid of any objective existence – of a representation. In the terminology of medieval logicians, which significantly reverses that of the moderns, the *esse subiectivum* of the *hupokeimenon* and of Aristotle's primary substance is replaced by the *esse obiectivum*: being in a representation. Thus begins the process that gradually but inflexibly transforms the theory of being into a doctrine of knowledge, ontology into gnoseology. Metaphysics no longer queries being but the conditions of its knowledge; no longer the structure of the world but the structure of knowledge. In Baumgarten's definition, "[m]etaphysics is the first science, because it contains the principles of all human knowledge" (*scientia prima cognitionis humanae principia continens*).[39] If being, like "thing" and the other transcendental terms, enters metaphysics only as the correlate of a representation and principle of knowledge, then the wonder about why something exists quickly gives way to knowledge and science. This exclusively gnoseological tendency, having reached critical mass in Kant, is what moved Heidegger to argue against it, by recasting the question of being.

The problem that remains unaddressed here really is the way our representations refer to an object. The medieval theorists seem to take this capacity for granted. Representation has an objective reality in itself, which does not coincide directly with the real being, and yet its connection with it remains unquestioned. No wonder that Kant's recasting of the problem of metaphysics would begin by asking what founds the relationship between our representations and objects; nor is it surprising that he sought an answer, perhaps in vain, in a transcendental philosophy.

It has been observed that medieval scholasticism, starting from Duns Scotus, "dissociates the question of the first object of the intellect from that of the subject of metaphysics"[40] and substitutes Henry of Ghent's *res* as the most general object of cognition with a purely linguistic reality, which it calls *quid nominis* or "being signifiable with a name" (*esse significabile per nomen*). According to Didier Demange, however, Duns Scotus did not in any way intend to identify this general concept with the object of metaphysics. "It makes metaphysics possible, without giving it a foundation, but opening a space for itself – semantics – into which it can insert itself."[41] This observation, although pertinent in itself, needs to be amended, in the sense that the medieval philosophers' lack of awareness about the unavoidable implication between semantics and metaphysics prevented them from bringing the problem of first philosophy's object fully into focus. Fourteenth-century philosophers offer an extremely subtle analysis of language's *modi significandi* ("modes of signifying"), an analysis that coexists alongside strictly ontological definitions; but an awareness of their inherent belonging together is not always quite as clear. Although Henry of Ghent and Buridan both seem to understand "thing" as something tied essentially to the *modus significandi* of the name, they do not draw all the consequences of this implication between linguistic representation and intellectual representation, language and thought. The ambiguity of *res*, which never fades away entirely despite the painstaking clarity of the distinctions, is rooted in this lack of awareness. The problem is clarified if we bring it back to the distinction between signification and denotation: through the

First Philosophy Last Philosophy

transcendental, metaphysics conceptualizes the status of being and reality proper to the meaning of the terms, independently of their denotation. But if the issue here is only a term's meaning, namely the relationship between the word and its representation, what ensures that the representation refers to a real object, that it has a denotation in discourse?

4
The Infinite Name

1. Every study in the history of thought must move constantly on two inseparable planes: the definition of the problem and the identification of the associated conceptuality. An exposition of the problem without the concepts that enable it to be articulated is just as sterile as a description of the concepts without the problem they refer to. My analysis of the conceptuality of first philosophy and metaphysics thus acquired a new sense once I attempted to place it in the problematic context of the unity and division of western knowledge. The questions we must then ask ourselves at this point are: what is the problem within which the transcendental conceptuality performs its crucial function? In which problematic context should we situate the slippage of being into the sphere of the thing?

A helpful clue for answering these questions comes from the fact that one of the first occurrences of the transcendental terms is in the treatises of the so-called *Logica modernorum*, as early as the first half of the thirteenth century. Here the context of the conceptuality of the transcendentals – especially *res* and *aliquid* – is the problem of "infinite names": the making infinite or "infinitization" (*infinitatio*) of logical terms. In the commentary on Aristotle's *De interpretatione* by Peter of Ireland (fl. c.1200–1260), Aquinas' teacher in Naples, we read: "It may be doubted whether the transcendental names, such as one, being, and something, can be made infinite [*possint infinitari*], since they are convertible, and this does not seem possible [. . .] and, indeed, it is impossible to make these transcendental names infinite."[1] But a few decades earlier the neologism *infinitari* appears passingly in Stephen Langton's (1150–1228) *Summa*, in the peremptory assertion that it is not possible to make the signified of the term *res* more infinite, because any denotation would be lost to it: *hoc nomen res non potest infinitari propter defectum suppositionis.*[2]

The expression "infinite name" (or "indefinite name") comes from a passage in Aristotle's *De interpretatione* (16a30): "'Not man' [*ouk anthrōpos*] is not a name, and there is no name by which it should be called. It is neither a statement nor a negation. Let us call it an indefinite name [*onoma aoriston*]" (in Boethius' translation, *nomen infinitum*, "infinite name"). The achievement of the medieval logicians was to transform Aristotle's infinite name into the problem of the limit to which the indeterminacy of a name's signified can be pushed, the limit beyond which every signified vanishes. The transcendentals are of course terms that cannot be made infinite because their signified is already so common and general that the addition of negation (*non res, non ens, non aliquid*) simply fails to denote. While through the negation contained in the infinite term 'not man' one can understand both being and nonbeing, "to

---

make 'being' and 'one' and 'something' infinite indicates nothing," as we read in Roger Bacon's *Summulae dialectices*, "nor can anything be understood by them if I say 'not being,' 'not something.' But this is not because of the force of the negation, but because of what the things signified by the term have in common, because it is common to all things that are, and so its privation is found only in a nonbeing."[3] And regarding "infinitized words," *Tractatus Anagnini*, composed a few decades earlier, states: "Of these it is necessary to know that an infinitized word [*vox infinitata*] is one that receives a negative particle to enter into a discursive composition. The nature of infinite terms is that they always want to attribute something to something. But the terms that already contain everything [*omnia continentes*] cannot be made more infinite. Consequently, to say 'not something is' or 'not thing is' [*non-aliquid est, non-res est*] is to say nothing [*nichil est*]."[4] Albert the Great was able at this point to state in his *Summa* the theorem that "thing, one, something, and being are infinite terms and therefore cannot be infinitized" (*infinitari non possunt*).[5]

The hypothesis I am suggesting here is that, before being was situated traditionally in the field of metaphysics and ontology, the conceptuality of the transcendentals had to do with the logical problem of infinitization, that is, the furthest limit of indeterminacy that linguistic signification can reach. At this threshold, the problem of the transcendentals borders on that of the signified of mathematical terms.

In an infinitized name, signification is brought to the edge of nothingness. From this perspective, the transcendental can be defined as the dimension of meaning that borders on nothingness, on Henry of Ghent's *purum nihil*. In *What Is Metaphysics?*, when

Heidegger formulates the fundamental problem of metaphysics as the question "Why is there something rather than nothing?" and asserts that being as a figure of nothingness remains forgotten in it, in reality this question makes sense only on the basis of the fact that metaphysics entered into the dimension of the transcendental and was henceforth inseparable from it. If the nothing "unveils itself as belonging to the being of beings,"[6] this is because, as transcendentals, being and the "thing" are at the limit of intelligibility only through their relationship – both of exclusion and of inclusion – with the nothing. The ultimate sense of the "thing" is that it is not-nothing, just as "[t]he nothing does not merely serve as the counterconcept [*Gegenbegriff*] of beings"[7] but belongs to them constitutively.

2.   A significant clue to the relationship between the terminology of metaphysics and that of mathematics lies the fact that in the Latin translations of the thirteenth-century Arab treatises of John of Seville, Gerard of Cremona, and Leonardo of Pisa the word used for the unknown (*shay* in Arabic, the same term that, along with *ens*, designates the first object of knowledge in Avicenna) is *res*.[8] Starting with Luca Pacioli's *Summa de arithmetica* (1494), the term is commonly translated in the vernacular as *cosa* (or *cossa*), that is, "thing": "from which it seemed to the first inventors that *cosa* should be understood of quantity, whatsoever it may be."[9] Girolamo Cardano, in his *Practica arithmetica*, thus lists among the denominative numbers (*numeri denominativi*, called numbers only *per similitudinem*, since they are not numbers but express variable quantities) *res sive radix sive la cosa* ("thing or root or the thing") adding: *et designatur: co* ("and it [i.e. any of them] is designated by the symbol *co*").[10] The Italian term gained such ground that it appeared even in algebra treatises in German, where it took the form *die Coss*.

Accordingly, reprinting Christian Rudolf's handbook of arithmetic under the title *Die Coss*, Stifel explained that an unknown quantity was called *Coss*, for which older authors used the expression *ponatur una res* (let a thing be posited).[11] And in his *Arithmetica integra* (1544) he shows awareness of the peculiarity of algebraic numbers, which are not truly numbers but rather algorithms: "The rule of algebra is such that it requires particular numbers, which must have an algorithm of their own" (*qui proprium Algorithmum habeant*).[12]

The fact that mathematicians were perfectly aware of the semantic implications of the term is evident in one of the most authoritative texts on the subject, Rafael Bombelli's *Algebra* (1572), which suggests that the "most universal and common" word *cosa* be replaced with the more precise *Tanti* ("so much, some amount"): "Some may be surprised that, contrary to the ancient usage of Italian writers who have written about this science of arithmetic, until this day when it fell to them to deal with an unknown quantity, they always named it using this word *cosa* as a word common to all unknown things, and I now call these quantities *Tanti*. But anyone who considers the matter properly will realize that this word *Tanto* is more appropriate to it than *cosa*, because if we say that *Tanto* is a word appropriate to number quantity, which cannot be said of *cosa*, since that word is most universal and common to all substances known and unknown [. . .], then *Tanto* is an unknown quantity by which at the end of the operation a number is found that is equal to it."[13]

It is no mere coincidence that the term designating the object of first philosophy is the same as the one used by mathematicians for unknown quantities. The object of metaphysics, reduced in the transcendental *res* to the empty correlate of a "bare precognition," had become so indeterminate that almost nothing separated it from the algebraic concept of the unknown. In this sense, the theory of the "thing" marks a threshold in which the conceptuality of metaphysics and mathematics would seem to overlap.

In Jacob Klein's admirable studies on ancient Greek logic and the birth of algebra, he stresses the conceptual differences that separate Greek mathematics from modern algebra (as developed by François Viète, Simon Stevin, and René Descartes). According to Klein, for the ancient Greeks a number is always "a number of something" (*arithmos tinos*), and the objects understood through the number are always determinate quantities. Even when Diophantus (third century BCE) develops the concept of unknown number, defined as "a number having in itself an indeterminate quantity of monads," the assumption is that the problem makes sense only if a precise number of monads represent the solution.[14] Regardless of how one envisages the transition from ancient Greek mathematics to modern algebra, the hypothesis we can entertain at this point is that this transition was made possible by the fact that, through the transcendental "thing," medieval metaphysics had for its part developed the concept of a general object as the furthest limit of linguistic signification. The algebraic number as an indeterminate "magnitude in general," which can be arrived at only through a symbolic procedure, had its predecessor in the transcendental doctrine of the "thing."

3. Let us try to delve deeper into the sphere of meaning of "thing" as an unknown algebraic term and as a transcendental term. Medieval theory distinguishes between signification (*significatio*) and supposition (*suppositio* – denotation, in modern terms). Signification is a property of the individual word (*vox*) in itself; supposition

belongs to a word insofar as it is placed in a proposition. "Supposition and signification differ," writes Petrus Hispanus, "since signification results from the imposition of a word to signify something [*per impositionem vocis ad rem significandam*]. Supposition, on the other hand, is the sense of a term that already in itself signifies a determinate thing, as when one says 'a man runs,' the term 'man' supposits for Socrates or Plato. Signification precedes supposition and they are different, because signifying pertains to a word, supposing [denoting] to a term already composed of word and signification."[15] Ockham distinguishes three forms of supposition: (1) material supposition, in which the word "supposits for itself [*supponit pro seipso*] but does not signify itself," as in the phrase "man is a name"; (2) simple supposition, in which the word supposits for a representation in the mind (*intentio animae*) but does not signify it, as in the phrase "man is a species"; (3) and personal supposition, "when a word supposits for the thing it signifies" (*supponit pro suo significato*), as in the phrase "a man – or this man – runs."[16] In the first two cases, supposition and signification remain separate, whereas in the third they coincide.

A careful look at the algebraic term *cosa* and the transcendental homonym suffices to ascertain that they do not fall under any of the three forms of supposition defined by Ockham. Insofar as the unknown is not a number but an algorithm, it does not refer to a determinate number but only to the fact that at the end of the operation there may be "a number that is equal to it." Similarly, the transcendent term *cosa* does not designate an existing thing, but the occurrence of a linguistic or mental representation in general, independently of the existence of its object. For this reason, *cosa* neither signifies nor supposits but means, so to speak, the disconnection itself between signification and denotation.

In an important passage in *Ordinatio*,[17] Duns Scotus distinguishes between *quid nominis*, the meaning sphere of the name, and being or *quid rei*, the thing insofar as it exists: "Yet, the 'what it is' of a name is more common than the being (*esse*) and than the 'what' of a thing because being signified by a name applies to more things than does being" (*Esse quid nominis est communius quam esse et quam quid rei, quia pluribus convenit significari nomine quam esse*). This singular theorem is worth reflecting upon. Duns Scotus states unreservedly that signification of the name exceeds being, like what Lévi-Strauss would define many centuries later as the irreducible excess of the signifier over the signified, which produces free or floating signifiers that are in themselves empty of meaning. Signification intrinsically exceeds its fulfilment through a denotation, just as the sphere of the *quid nominis* in every case surpasses that of the *quid rei*. The algebraic thing and the thing as a transcendental term are situated in this gap between signification and supposition.

At this point, it can be hypothesized that at the base of the transcendental predicates lies something like an architranscendental presupposition, which coincides with what, with reference to Aristotle's *pros hen*, we have called the "being-said." In Duns Scotus' terms, it corresponds to the *quid nominis*, the pure fact of being said and named in language. This architranscendental, which is logically prior to the "thing," emerges in the awareness of these philosophers only indirectly, and yet somehow remains presupposed in their definitions.

4. To bridge this gap between signification and denotation, the medieval logicians introduced the concept, giving it an eminent position. The foundations of the problem lay in the semantic plexus that Aristotle's *Peri hermeneias* (*De interpretatione*) had established between words, things, and the affections of the soul. Ancient commentators had already wondered which of these three elements the text referred to. Their answer was that it dealt with words insofar as they designate things through the affections of the soul. In Boethius' commentary, this interpretation moves toward giving primacy to what he defines as conceptions of the soul, or intellections (which will later become "concepts"): "the word," he writes, "signifies the conceptions of the soul or intellections" (*vox vero conceptiones animi intellectusque significat*), and it refers to things only "by means of these, in a secondary way" (*secundaria significatione per intellectum medietate*).[18]

Ockham and the medieval logicians systemized this notion and placed the concept firmly at the center of the logico-linguistic plexus. Ockham thus distinguishes the *terminus conceptus*, the conceptual term, from the spoken and written word, defining it as "an intention or affection [impression] of the soul which signifies or consignifies something naturally and is intended to be part of a mental proposition" (*aliquid naturaliter significans vel consignificans, nata esse pars propositioni mentalis*).[19] With a reversal of the order implicit in Aristotle's statement, which began with spoken words (*ta en tēi phonēi*), the concept and the mental proposition to which it belongs precede the spoken proposition. "Thus, whenever anyone utters a spoken proposition, he forms beforehand a mental proposition. This proposition is internal and it belongs to no particular spoken language. [. . .] The parts of such mental propositions are called concepts, intentions, likenesses, and 'intellects.'"[20]

Ockham's theory of the *suppositio personalis* acquires its proper meaning on the basis of this primacy of the concept. The concept or intention naturally signifies something that can also denote (*est quoddam in anima, quod est signum naturaliter significans aliquid, pro quo potest supponere*).[21] Since in his theory the concept denotes that which it signifies (*supponit pro suo significato*), the *suppositio personalis* stands as a canon of logico-linguistic signification, of which simple and material denotation are but subclasses. The spoken word – which in reality always also contains a *suppositio materialis*, a reference to its material substance – is thus effectively eliminated and replaced by the concept.

A notion of this kind, whose logico-linguistic plexus resides most notably in the *conceptus mentis* and not in a problematic relationship between word and thing, paves the way to that "de-linguisticization" (*Entsprachlichung*) of knowledge that Ruprecht Paqué, in an exceptional book,[22] saw as a condition of possibility for modern science. If the ancients were neither able nor willing to access science in the modern sense of the word, this is because, despite the development of mathematics (significantly not in algebraic form), their experience of language and their ontology did not allow them to refer to the world independently of the way it is revealed in language. Conversely, when the word is fully resolved in the concept, as it is in medieval logic, an avenue opens to a form of knowledge that can do without words and substitute algorithms and numbers for natural languages. This is what the transcendental "thing" expresses: an immediate relationship between word and concept. As Ockham and Buridan suggest, *ens in quantum ens* means "the term *ens* insofar as it is resolved in the concept *ens*." From this perspective, every linguistic term is therefore ultimately a *terminus conceptus*, which denotes that which it signifies. The theory of transcendentals, far from confusing logic with reality, as Kant believed, implies a logic and an experience of language that prepares access to a Newtonian science, whose metaphysical foundations, it has been suggested,[23] Kant aimed to secure on his own terms.

Conceptus appears as a technical term in Priscian (fifth century). In his *Institutiones grammaticae*, a founding text for medieval thought on language, we read that "whenever speech that signifies something is uttered [*quaecumque igitur vox literata profertur significans aliquid*], a word that indicates the mind's concept – that is, a thought [*vox indicans mentis conceptum, id est cogitationem*] – must be called a part of speech [*pars orationis*]."[24] The term conveys metaphorically its original, physiological meaning (the fetus conceived in the womb), which is still evident in Macrobius: "Advice is born from a conception of the mind" (*conceptu mentis consilia nascuntur*).[25] The term was then adopted by a group of thirteenth-century logicians and grammarians known as Modists, in whom reflection on grammar and reflection on philosophy were so close to each other that one of the questions debated was "whether modes of understanding, modes of signifying, and modes of being are entirely identical." The original meaning is still discernible in Aquinas, in chapter 3 of a treatise entitled *Reasons for Our Faith: Against the Muslims*: "Whenever the intellect actually understands, it forms a certain intelligible object, which is its offspring, so to speak, and for this reason is called a concept of the mind" (*Quandocumque autem actu intelligit, quoddam intelligibile format, quod est quasi quaedam proles ipsius, unde et mentis conceptus nominatur*). It is this

---

"offspring of the mind," invented by a fifth-century grammarian, that, through a long historical process culminating with Hegel, would gradually become the true object of philosophy.

5. Connected to concept in its capacity as element of mental discourse is the theme of representation, which so thoroughly marked thirteenth- and fourteenth-century thought that from then on, it has been said, modern metaphysics became a theory of representation. Although the word appeared earlier, in Tertullian and Augustine, only in that period did *repraesentatio* and *repraesentare* become fundamental technical terms in the philosophical lexicon, especially with Duns Scotus and his school. This primacy of representation played an essential role in the displacement of metaphysics from doctrine of being into doctrine of knowledge, a process I have mentioned several times. The impressions on the soul (*en tēi psuchēi pathēmata*) from Aristotle's *De interpretatione* are not actually representations in the sense of medieval logic but simply "likenesses" (*homoiōmata*) of things, likenesses that depend on these things. When Aquinas, in his *Commentary on Peter Lombard's Sentences*, analyzes the intellect's conceptuality regarding things, he is careful to distinguish the thing's simple likeness, which exists outside the soul (*similitudo rei existentis extra animam*), from *conceptio*, which does not refer immediately to the thing but rather to the way of understanding it (*ex modo intelligendi rem*). And he adds "about this species, it is the intentions that our understanding discovers" (*intentiones quas intellectus noster adinvenit*) (*Sent.* I, d. 2, q. I, a. 3). These representations arise from the fact that "the intellect, reflecting on itself, just as it understands things

existing outside the soul, understands them insofar as they are understood" (*ex hoc enim quod intellectus in se ipsum reflectitur, sicut intelligit res existentes extra animam, ita intelligit eas esse intellectas*) (*De potentia*, q. VII, a. 6). For Aquinas, however, even these, which he calls "second intentions," despite having their immediate foundation in the intellect and not in the thing, do maintain a remote foundation in the thing.

With Duns Scotus, the status of representation is further developed. Unlike the senses, the intellect does not require the real presence of an object that imprints its species on the sense organs; rather the object is present in the intellect, in potency, before the act of intellection, "not as the impression in an organ" (the intellect has no organs) "but by an impression in the cognitive potency: such a representative impression, which precedes the act of intelligence in potency, I call intelligible species."[26] This particular presence is defined as an "intentional affection" distinct from real affection and compared to the light that the object emanates as it shines forth in the species (*relucet in specie*): "The intellect does not really undergo an affection from the real object, which imprints a real species, but undergoes an intentional affection [*patitur passione intentionali*] from the object insofar as it shines forth in the species; and this second passion is the receptivity of the intelligence, which proceeds from the intelligible insofar as it is intelligible and shines forth in the intelligible species, and this undergoing [of an affection] is the intellection."[27] "Therefore," concludes Duns Scotus, "in the cognitive potency, one perfection does not depend on another but may have its object present in itself independently of any other potency."[28] Representation has its own ontological

———

status, which Scotus and his pupils call "intentional being," distinct from real being and defined as the being "which agrees with the thing insofar as it exists representatively [*repraesentative*] and has a being represented in another being." In the work of Duns Scotus' brilliant pupil William of Alnwick, to whom we owe the definition just cited, representation (the "representing form") is identical to the represented being of the object and to the intelligibility that accompanies the creature from time immemorial (*esse repraesentatum obiecti representati est idem realiter cum forma repraesentante*). And this intelligibility has a theological foundation, since it is ultimately identified with God (*teneo quod esse intelligibile creaturae ab aeterno est idem realiter cum Deo*).[29]

Although there are authors who question the very existence of representation in the mind as a useless intermediary between the object and the intellect, the intentional being, in its connection with the concept, would have a long lineage in western philosophy, persisting at least as far Husserl and Brentano.

6.   Let me try to set out the results of this archaeological summary of the transcendental in a few points, or at least flesh out my hypothesis according to which the transcendental terms of medieval logic are, more or less consciously, the correlate of the intentionality of language. In this sense they do not define a supreme genus, more general than the categories, but rather result from the very fact that language exists. While the categories order and delimit what is said through names (the unconnected *legomena*), the transcendental terms correspond to the very fact that one says, that names are given; but "that one says" is in no way a more common

and general predicate than the said. Accordingly, one might say that the proper place of the transcendental is in the gap between signification and denotation. If my hypothesis is correct, the transcendentals express, without consciously focusing on it, the same relationship between language and the world, between our representations and things.

In the history of metaphysics, however, this relationship has been interpreted as the most general and most common signified: the "thing" as the extreme edge of signification. The experience of being *haplōs* as something that responds to the pure existence of language is displaced in the ultimate, most liminal dimension that thought can possibly reach. As Wilhelm Dilthey showed, the metaphysical concept of substance (*ousia*) is, from this point of view, nothing but a development of the concept of thing.[30] In the transcendental, language reaches a threshold beyond which there is no more signified, except for the pure fact that there is signification, that there is a bare relationship between representations and things, independently of any denotation. This is why these transcendental terms cannot be made infinite and why they border on the nothing.

The excess of the signifier (*quid nominis*) over the signified (*quid rei*) theorized by Duns Scotus finds its place on this threshold – and with that the scope of its validity, too. The attempt to maintain the current conception of language as a signifying voice at this ambiguous, extreme edge is at the root of the aporias to which the transcendental condemns thought. To return the transcendental to its proper place would require nothing less than a conception of language radically different from the one that has dominated our culture at least since Aristotle's *De interpretatione*. In this conception, the character proper to language is defined through the interweaving of words, concepts (affections or impressions of the soul), and things. Words are *sēmantika*, signifying, because through concepts they signify things and can refer to things (that is, have a denotation); because concepts, of which words are signs, are in their turn likenesses (*omoiōmata*) of things. According to this conception, neither the relationship of signification between words and concepts nor the relationship between concepts and things is in any way explained. The entirely arbitrary intervention of the letter – (*gramma*) as a kind of *deus ex machina*, which, by articulating the word, allows it to signify – betrays the groundlessness of a conception of language that philosophy has attempted to call into question only during the last century. And it is no accident that, in a letter to Marcus Herz where he evokes the mystery at the origin of his inquiry, "the whole secret of the metaphysics that had until then remained hidden to itself," Kant expresses it in a question: "on what grounds rests the reference of what in us is called representation [*Vorstellung*] to the object [*Gegenstand*]?"[31] And in *Cratylus* (422d) Plato asked, no less resolutely: "Well, then, how can the earliest names, which are not as yet based upon any others, make clear to us the nature of things?" The experience of language that takes place here does not signify or denote; it names and it calls.

At issue here along with this conception is the dogma of intentionality, which is at work ceaselessly from Aristotle to Husserl and according to which every thought and all speech always refer to something. In this sense being, too, is something: the something, the *aliquid*, the *Etwas*, or the *ti* that thought and language, pushed to the furthest transcendental threshold, cannot but continue to say and think. It must be affirmed instead that, insofar as it is situated in the gap between signification and denotation, the thought that language may represent, or "that which gets said," is wholly devoid of any intentionality; it is not a thought or a *logos* of *something*. What it corresponds to is not a limit dimension of signification, not even in the mystical form of a negation or a dark night, but an experience absolutely heterogeneous to that: not a logic but an ethics; not a *logos* but an *ethos* or a form of life. In other words, ethics is first and foremost the experience that reveals itself when we dwell in a fully nonintentional language. Far from being mute and ineffable, it is the speech we find when language frees itself from its suppositional and pre-suppositional pretension and addresses itself not as the object of a metalanguage but as the rhythm and scansion of a doing, a *poiēsis*.

The final pages of Dilthey's *Introduction to the Human Sciences* are dedicated to the dissolution of the metaphysical attitude in modernity. In them, he shows that metaphysics can find nothing in reality but a logical nexus. He also shows that there is an idea beyond which metaphysics cannot proceed in its attempt to connect to a representable whole the ultimate concepts at which the natural sciences arrive: that of a "conceivability" in general, which is nothing but "an abstract expression for *the imaginable*" [*rappresentabilità*].[32] Our archaeological summary of the transcendental has led us to similar conclusions. Having become "the queen of a shadow realm," metaphysics resolves into epistemology and into a doctrine of science. According to Dilthey, this transformation of the world into the subject that knows it coincides with "the euthanasia of philosophy."[33] The transcendental concepts of "thing," "conceivability," and "imaginability [*rappresentabilità*]" are actually empty. They cannot ensure any dominion of metaphysics over the natural sciences: ultimately, they can only surrender the field to a new, positivistic metaphysics, which substitutes atoms and elementary particles for substance. All the more, then, must they yield to a knowledge that purely and simply gives up on any logical representation of the world, as happens in post-quantum physics.

5
The Transcendental
Object = X

1. Three terms reappear in the conceptual fabric of Kant's *Critique of Pure Reason*, overlapping and criss-crossing one another at every turn: pure, *a priori*, and transcendental. The adjective "pure" (*rein*) makes its first appearance in the *Critique* – apart from in the title – in the preface to the first edition, when Kant announces his desire to establish a court of justice (*Gerichtshof*) through which reason can secure its legitimate claims and condemn those that are groundless: "this court is none other than the critique of pure reason itself."[1] Immediately afterwards, he explains what we are meant to understand here by "purity": pure is a cognition "independent of all experience." And, against those who claim to extend human reason beyond all limits of possible experience (*über alle Grenze möglicher Erfahrung*), he adds, to avoid confusion: "I humbly admit that this wholly surpasses my capacity; instead I have to do merely with reason itself and its pure thinking" (*ihrem reinen denken*).[2] If "pure concepts of understanding" and a "pure understanding," are mentioned later, their

purity is defined once again with respect to experience: "the chief question always remains: 'What and how much can understanding and reason cognize free of all experience?'"[3] ("free" [*frei*] is juxtaposed here to the "beyond" [*über*] of those who wish to surmount the limits of possible experience).

Taken in this sense, the term "pure" seems to coincide with *a priori*: "Pure reason," the Introduction states, "is that which contains the principles for cognizing something absolutely *a priori*."[4] However, earlier on, the relationship between the two terms had been further clarified: *a priori* cognitions are those that "occur *absolutely* independently of all experience. [. . .] Among *a priori* cognitions, however, those are called pure with which nothing empirical is intermixed."[5]

Immediately after defining pure reason through *a priori* cognition, Kant introduces the concept of transcendental, which is closely connected to the previous two terms: "I call all cognition transcendental that is occupied not so much with objects but with our manner of cognition of objects insofar as this is to be possible *a priori*."[6] "A system of such concepts" – all the concepts of pure reason – "would be called transcendental philosophy."[7] Kant strives meticulously to distinguish what seems to coincide at each instance: "not every *a priori* cognition must be called transcendental, but only that by means of which we cognize that and how certain representations (intuitions or concepts) are applied entirely *a priori*, or are possible (i.e., the possibility of cognition or its use [*der Gebrauch*] *a priori*)."[8]

The subtlety of this distinction cannot always be maintained. Thus, after providing a table of categories, of the pure concepts of the understanding, Kant

states that they have a "merely transcendental significance (*Bedeutung*), but are not of any transcendental
use"[9] ("merely" or rather "nudely," according to the
primary meaning of the adjective *bloss*, which is used
here adverbially). On the contrary, he explains a few
lines later, "since (as merely pure categories [*bloss reine
Kategorien*]) they are not supposed to have empirical
use, and cannot have transcendental use, they do not
have any use at all [*von gar keinem Gebrauch*] if they
are separated from all sensibility, i.e., they cannot be
applied to any supposed object at all; rather they are
merely [*bloss* again] the pure form of the use of the
understanding in regard to objects in general and of
thinking, yet without any sort of object being able to be
thought or determined through them alone."[10] A little
earlier, though, Kant had evoked precisely such an
impossible "transcendental use" regarding something
that he called a bare transcendental object ("Thinking
is the action of relating given intuitions to an object. If
the manner of this intuition is not given in any way, then
the object [*der Gegenstand*] is merely [*bloss*] transcendental, and the concept of the understanding has none
other than a transcendental use"[11]).

2. It is the status of this paradoxical "transcendental object" that we must attempt to define, because at
issue here is precisely that "distinction of all objects
in general into phenomena and noumena" that lends
the chapter its name. Transcendental means here that,
since every sensible intuition has been abstracted, in it
"no object is determined, rather only the thought of an
object in general is expressed in accordance with different *modi*."[12]

In the first edition, the passage quoted here continued by explaining how the distinction between phenomena and noumena (between the sensible world and the intelligible world) was founded on the fact that our understanding tends to refer our representations illegitimately to the concept of something in general, which is "to that extent only the transcendental object." "This signifies, however, a something = X," Kant explains, "of which we know nothing at all nor can know anything in general (in accordance with the current constitution of our understanding), but is rather something that can serve only as a correlate of the unity of apperception."[13] Such a "transcendental object" is nothing but "the entirely undetermined thought of something in general" (*Etwas überhaupt*). And this "cannot be called the *noumenon*; for I do not know anything about what it is in itself, and have no concept of it except merely [*bloss*] that of the object of a sensible intuition in general, which is therefore the same for all appearances."[14] The understanding is misled into ambiguity (*Zweideutigkeit*): it confuses "the entirely undetermined concept of a being of understanding [*Verstandwesen*], as a something in general outside of our sensibility."[15]

Clearly the "object in general = X" corresponds exactly to what the medieval logicians conceived of as the transcendental "thing" (*res a reor*, distinct from *res rata* – from the real thing or, in Kantian terms, from an intuition given by sensibility). This is all the more true as Kant's text becomes clearer if one relates it to Ockham's linguistic theory of signification. What Kant calls "transcendental significance" (*Bedeutung*) is the medieval logicians' *significatio*; and what he calls "use" is Ockham's *suppositio* (denotation). From the perspective of a linguistic analysis – which in Kant is quite lacking, as Hamann complains – the categories are actually terms that signify but do not denote. The mistake lies precisely in assuming a denotation (a reference to an object) where it cannot but be absent.

3. It is at this point that Kant introduces the concept of "an illusion that cannot be avoided at all" (*eine schwer zu vermeidende Täuschung*),[16] soon afterwards to become an inevitable "transcendental illusion," which "does not cease even though it is uncovered and its nullity is clearly seen into by transcendental criticism."[17] The cause of this illusion is that our reason mistakes subjective principles for an objective determination of things and claims to make, illegitimately, transcendental *use* of a concept that has only a transcendental *significance*. Kant then stresses once again the unavoidable and even natural character of this illusion (*natürliche und unvermeidliche Illusion*),[18] which is bound indissolubly to human reason and will therefore never cease "to lead our reason on with false hopes, continually propelling it into momentary aberrations" (*in Verirrungen zu stossen*, which is almost a direct quotation of Aristotle's "eternally aporetic," *aei aporoumenon*).[19]

Indeed, if we strip the pure concepts of the understanding of "the only one [sensible intuition] that is possible for us," they are only forms of thought (*Gedankenformen*), with which we are given no object. And yet the transcendental illusion pushes us to think, beyond sensible beings (*phaenomena*) and beyond intelligible beings (*noumena*) and claims to have a "kind of cognition."[20] "But right at the outset here there is an ambiguity [*Zweideutigkeit*], which can occasion great misunderstanding. Since the understanding, when it calls an object in a relation mere phenomenon, simultaneously makes for itself, beyond this relation, another representation of an object in itself [*Gegenstand an sich selbst*] [. . .] it is thereby misled into taking the entirely undetermined concept of a being of understanding, as a something in general [*einem Etwas überhaupt*] outside of our sensibility, for a determinate concept of a being that we could cognize through the understanding in some way."[21]

This is the perspective from which we must reread Kant's digression on "the transcendental philosophy of the ancients," which he introduced into the second edition of the *Critique of Pure Reason* immediately after providing the table of the categories. Whether or not Kant presents, as has been suggested,[22] a "definitive accounting" of scholastic metaphysics (especially in the form it reached in Baumgarten), it is certain that his intention was to show the heterogeneity and inadequacy of the scholastic transcendentals *ens, unum, verum, bonum* by comparison with his own deduction of the pure concepts of the understanding. "These supposedly transcendental predicates of things are nothing other than logical requisites and criteria of all cognition of things in general," which the ancients nevertheless took for properties of the things themselves.[23] They certainly do not complete the transcendental table of categories, almost as if it were incomplete. For this reason, they add nothing to it and, since the relationship of these concepts with objects was entirely brushed aside, they can only refer to the agreement that cognition has with itself.

One might wonder whether Kant's polemical impulse prevailed over historical objectivity. Scholastic philosophers such as Henry of Ghent and Buridan were perfectly aware of the distinction between forms of thought (*res a reor*) and real objects (*res rata*). And Kant believed that, if an ambiguity arose in them, it had to be a consequence of the transcendental illusion that he himself had declared to be unavoidable.

4. The problem that Kant tries to get to the bottom of is the unavoidable tendency of our understanding and language to refer to an object even when it is not there. In our representations, there is – or there seems to be – a capacity to refer to objects whose foundation is not easy to grasp. This is the problem that, in his letter of February 21, 1772 to Marcus Herz, he identifies as the starting point of his inquiries into metaphysics. "While I was thinking through the theoretical part in its whole extent and the reciprocal relations of its sections, I noticed that there was still something essential that was lacking, which I (like others) in my long metaphysical inquiries had failed to consider and which indeed constitutes the key to the whole secret of the metaphysics that had until then remained hidden to itself [*den Schlüssel zum ganzen Geheimnis der bis dahin sich selbst noch verborgenen Metaphysik ausmacht*]. I asked myself, namely: on what grounds rests the reference of what in us is called representation to the object? [*auf welchem Grund beruth die Beziehung desjenigen, was man in uns Vorstellungen nennt auf den Gegenstand*]."[24]

Answering this question would not be difficult if the representation contained only the mode of representation in which the subject is passively impressed by the object, or if what we call representation in us were instead active and produced the object.

"But," continues Kant, "neither is our understanding by means of its representations the cause of the object [through its representations] [. . .] nor is the object the cause of the representations of the understanding in the real sense (*in sensu reali*). The pure concepts of the understanding must, therefore, not be abstracted from the sensation of the senses, nor must those concepts express the receptivity of representations through sense; but they must, to be sure, have their sources in the nature of the soul, though not insofar as they are produced by the object nor insofar as they bring forth the object itself."[25]

Kant believes that he has responded to this question through the transcendental table of the pure concepts of the understanding. "While I was searching in such a way for the sources of intellectual cognition, without which the nature and the bounds of metaphysics cannot be determined, I reduced this science to its essentially distinct parts; and I sought to reduce transcendental philosophy, namely, all the concepts of completely pure reason, to a definite number of categories [*die Transzendentalphilosophie, nämlich alle Begriffe der gänzlich reinen Vernunft, in eine gewisse Zahl von Kategorien zu bringen*]."[26] Transcendental is here defined as philosophy, insofar as it deals with "completely pure reason," independent of experience. It has been pointed out, however, that in the letter Kant seems to refer to the use of these concepts in connection with the data of sensibility as well as to their use in connection with things in themselves. The transcendental is actually an ambiguous concept: it refers to the possibility of an *a priori* cognition, which, along with the sensibility, enables us to cognize the objects of experience, as much as to the transcendental object and the noumena, which are not objects but empty concepts of which no knowledge is possible. In other words, there is both a legitimate use of the transcendental, in relation to the data of sensibility, and an illegitimate use, which concerns "the bare transcendental object" and corresponds perfectly to the scholastics' supertranscendental.

Also transcendental is illusion, against which critique must remain vigilant: it makes us see an object where in reality there is nothing, and it purports to think where there is nothing left to think. No surprise, then, that the noumenon ranks first in the table of nothingness that concludes transcendental logic as *ens rationis* or "objectless empty concept," alongside simple negation (shadow, cold), *ens imaginarium* (space and time, which are not objects but forms of intuition), and pure and simple contradiction (for example, a two-sided rectilinear figure).[27] From a linguistic point of view, we are dealing with a term that, just like "thing" and the scholastics' supertranscendentals, has a meaning but not a use or a denotation.

The possibility or impossibility of a metaphysics in general, the problem Kant had set out to resolve, coincides with resolving the misunderstandings about itself to which reason had succumbed. Since "understanding and sensibility can determine an object only in combination" and, once separated, give rise only to "representations that we cannot relate to any determinate object,"[28] the critique must ensure that the pure concepts of understanding remain empty of any object and metaphysical terms remain devoid of denotation.

5.   There is nevertheless one area in which the noumenon performs a function that guarantees its necessity and ensures metaphysics – at one time "called the queen of all the sciences" – its legitimate royal claim.[29] This is its capacity "to limit the objective validity of sensible cognition" so that it does not extend its dominion into the realm of pure understanding. Kant's well-known definition of the noumenon – "merely a boundary concept

[*bloss ein Grenzbegriff*], in order to limit the pretension of sensibility" – should be understood in this way.[30] As far as it traces these impassable boundaries, the concept of noumenon, just like transcendental illusion, "remains not only admissible, but even unavoidable."[31]

On closer inspection, this means that the pure concepts of metaphysics, taken in themselves, are altogether empty and have no other purpose than to provide both a limit and a foundation for the specialized sciences: a foundation in their empirical use, if they are put in relation with sensible experience; a limit in their bare transcendental use, outside any relationship with sensibility. What the critique really establishes with certainty is that there are no objects other than those of experience (that is, ultimately, the objects of the sciences). The noumenon and the transcendental object are not objects, but rather the empty place where thought has literally nothing to think. Metaphysics makes sense only if, at each instance, it resolves a misunderstanding and an illusion from which it can never free itself, seeing that it is condemned to drift in a "stormy ocean, the true seat of illusion, where many a fog bank and rapidly melting iceberg pretend to be new lands."[32]

Once again, the primacy of the queen of all the sciences is simultaneously confirmed and restricted peremptorily to the advantage of the sciences. This explains why, a year before the second edition of the *Critique*, Kant published the *Metaphysical Foundations of Natural Science*, where we read in the preface that "[p]roperly so-called natural science presupposes, in the first place, metaphysics of nature" and "[a] rational doctrine of nature thus deserves the name of a natural science, only in case the fundamental natural laws therein are cognized a priori."[33] And yet in the preface to the second edition of the *Critique* (where the only proper names to appear are, apart from the incidental mention of Socrates, those of scientists: Galileo, Torricelli, Stahl, and Copernicus), he can take mathematics and physics as examples of the revolution that metaphysics must undergo if it is to put itself "onto the secure course of a science," onto which it has not yet had the "rare good fortune [*das Schicksal*, fate, destiny]" to be brought.[34]

This makes the singularity of Kant's gesture all the more remarkable. The transcendental is the fortress inside which metaphysics, faced with the unremitting progress of the sciences, has entrenched itself to somehow keep hold of its primacy over them, purporting in this way to both limit and found the scope of their validity. To do this, it had to empty itself of any reference to experience and to guard against the illusion that had led it perpetually to wander from its abandoned transcendental dwelling. What actually occurred, and could not but occur, is that the sciences continued in their unstoppable progress, with no regard for limits or foundations, and the queen had to accept that she had lost all control over her supposed subjects and vassals.

But there is one fact she could rejoice over: the sciences have ended up abiding more or less consciously by her prescriptions, at least on one point. Post-quantum physics has actually given up any claim of accessing the reality of things in themselves and has even postulated an interdependence between the researcher's actions and the phenomena he or she interacts with during the experiment. A meagre consolation, perhaps, considering that the very concept of reality has been sidelined and replaced by probability. The noumenon, which guarded the inviolable threshold of the thing in itself, real but unknown to us, has been replaced by an algorithm that acquires a presence during each experiment, a presence that is precise and random in equal measure.

Kant's transformation of metaphysics into the science of the cognitive conditions of possibility culminates in Fichte's *Wissenschaftslehre* ("theory of knowledge"). Philosophy, which seeks at all costs to affirm itself as science, can do so only by becoming "the science of science": "What was previously called 'philosophy' would therefore be called *the science of science as such*."[35] That the problem was now the status of philosophy vis-à-vis the newly developed natural sciences is evident from the thesis that metaphysics maintains its dominion over the system of sciences in the form of a "knowledge of knowledge" (*Wissenschaftslehre*). "The [doctrine of science], however, is not only supposed to provide itself with its own form; it is also supposed to supply the form of all possible additional sciences and it is supposed to establish the validity of this form for all the sciences."[36] The sciences are "are related to the *Wissenschaftslehre* in the same way that something established is related to the foundation upon which it is established."[37] At this point, all the aporias that accompanied first philosophy from Aristotle up to its establishment as a transcendental science rush back into view. If "there can be only one system in human knowledge,"[38] then "all those propositions that serve as foundational principles of the various particular sciences are, at the same time, propositions contained within the *Wissenschaftslehre*"[39] and there will no longer be particular sciences, "but merely parts of one and the same *Wissenschaftslehre*."[40] To exist as science in itself, however, the science of knowledge must be a science of something and consequently have its own object. But this object can only be the system of human knowledge in general.[41] The problem that philosophy would once again strive in vain to resolve was that of giving objective substance to something that cannot and must not be conceived of as an object.

6
The Metaphysical
Animal

1. An examination of how Aristotelian first philosophy has been received in the history of philosophy could have begun with its ending: with Heidegger's refoundation and overcoming of metaphysics, where the difficulties and contradictions of the problem seem to arrive at a defining junction. Heidegger's privileged relationship with Aristotle, whom he once characterized as "more Greek" than Plato, can be taken as a given. It is no surprise, then, that he tackled early on what he would label the onto-theological constitution of the Aristotelian metaphysics, and continued to do so until the later phase of his thought.

Already in his 1924–1925 course on Plato's *Sophist*, he sets the problem out clearly in its fundamental elements. Heidegger starts from Aristotle's thesis of a science that contemplates being qua being and immediately observes that there is a dual aspect to it from the beginning: "This idea of first philosophy, as Aristotle calls it, the original science of beings, is for him intersected by another fundamental science, which he designates as *theologikē.*"[1] Aristotle does not have the term "ontology," as the science of being qua being will later be called: "Thus theology as well as ontology claim to be *prōtē philosophia.*"[2] With a barely veiled allusion to the interpretations of Jaeger and Natorp, Heidegger describes any attempt to find a mediation between ontology and theology in Aristotle as "sterile." Rather, it is a matter of understanding "why Greek science travelled such a path that it landed, as it were, with these two basic sciences, ontology and theology."[3] These reasons coincide with the notion that ancient Greeks had of being as presence (*Anwesenheit*): for them, "Beings are what is present in the proper sense." If the theme of ontology is the presence of being in general, "not tailored to a definite region," theology instead considers beings "according to what they are already in advance, i.e., according to what constitutes, in the most proper and highest sense, the presence of the world."[4] There is no contradiction, then, in the dual articulation of first philosophy: "The development of Greek science is pursued in these two original dimensions of reflection on Being." The problem does not lie so much in the appearance of theology, "whose approach is relatively clear to us, as it was to the Greeks as well," as in ontology itself, since it requires us to question in every instance the relationship between universal characteristics, which pertain to all beings qua beings, and the individual concrete being. What appears in this questioning, therefore, is nothing less than the problem of the ontological difference between Being and beings, which would become one of the main themes in Heidegger's thought. But "the basic questioning of ontology, from Aristotle and the Greeks up to the present, shows that we have in fact not advanced one step forward; indeed, quite to the contrary, the position the Greeks attained has for us been lost and we therefore do not even understand these questions any longer."[5]

It is significant that, shortly before this, Heidegger poses the problem of the relationship between first philosophy and the other sciences. Commenting on Aristotle's assertion that the science of being qua being is different from the so-called particular (*en merēi*) sciences, which carve out a part of being and examine its accidents, he consequently describes the relationship between first philosophy and the other sciences in a way that remains constant throughout his thought. "Here are sciences which cut out, from the whole of beings, determined regions and then address those regions purely as delimited in themselves, elaborating them in *legein*. Every such science has, as we say, its determined region. To the regions of these sciences there corresponds a definite *aisthēsis*, an original perception in which the fundamental character of the objects in the region is grasped, either explicitly or not. In geometry, the objects are the relations of space or site, which are not at all given with Being as such; the objects of *phusikē* are beings insofar as they are in motion."[6] Instead of taking this determination of the relationship between metaphysics and the particular sciences for granted, we must question it.

2. In his 1926 course *Basic Concepts of Ancient Philosophy*, in opposition to Jaeger, who argued that "Aristotle was here not equal to the problem of Being," Heidegger asserts that the double concept (*Doppelbegriff*) of first philosophy is "steadfastly consistent."[7] The

positing of a science of beings qua beings "necessarily includes the question of the particular being in which genuine Being is most purely demonstrated. [...] Whether this being is the first mover or the first heaven is a secondary question." Theology "is not a special science; on the contrary, it is an ontologically oriented science. It is the science of that which Being genuinely means and also the science of that being which genuinely is; science of Being and of the highest being."[8]

In his 1928 course, *The Metaphysical Foundations of Logic*, the twofold character of first philosophy is emphasized once again and, at the same time, further problematized: "[I]s philosophy either an ontology or a theology? Or is it both at once? Does that which is sought under the term 'theology' in fact reside in the essence of philosophy understood totally and radically? Or is what arises in Aristotle as theology still a remnant of his early period? [...] These questions cannot be resolved solely through historical–philological interpretation. On the contrary, this interpretation itself requires that we be guided by an understanding of the problem which is a match for what is handed down. And we must first acquire such an understanding."[9]

What that understanding may be is suggested later, with reference to the place of a fundamental ontology in *Being and Time*, namely through the difference between Being and beings and the relationship between Dasein and being: "The intrinsic necessity for ontology to turn back to its point of origin can be clarified by reference to the primal phenomenon of human existence: the being 'man' understands being; understanding-of-being effects a distinction between being and beings; being is there only when Dasein understands being."[10]

The definition of metaphysics as onto-theology appears in his 1930–1931 course, *Hegel's Phenomenology of Spirit*. Here Aristotle is mentioned in the context of an interpretation of Hegel, but it is crucial to note that "[t]he expression 'onto-theo-logy' should not point to a connection with a discipline called 'theology,' but should indicate to us the most central thrust of the problem of being."[11] As he explained in the earlier 1927 course *The Basic Problems of Phenomenology*, the Aristotelian definition of first philosophy as theology "has nothing to do with the present-day concept of Christian theology as a positive science. They have only the name in common."[12]

In the course on Hegel, Heidegger is unreservedly critical of the traditional way in which the relationship between philosophy and science has been understood. "But why is philosophy called *the* science? We are inclined – because of custom – to answer this question by saying that philosophy provides the existing or possible sciences with their foundations, i.e., with a determination and possibility of their fields (e.g., nature and history), as well as with the justification of their procedures. By providing all sciences with their foundation, philosophy must certainly be science. For philosophy cannot be less than what originates from it – the sciences. This view of philosophy, which has flourished since Descartes, has been more or less clearly and thoroughly developed. It attempted to justify itself with recourse to ancient philosophy, which also conceived of itself as a knowing, indeed as the highest knowledge. This concept of philosophy as *the* science became increasingly dominant from the nineteenth century to the present. This took place, not on the basis of the inner wealth and original impulses of philosophizing, but rather – as in neo-Kantianism – out of perplexity over the proper task of philosophy. It appears to have been deprived of this perplexity because the sciences have occupied all fields of reality. Thus, nothing was left for philosophy except to become the science of these sciences."[13]

———

The critique does not spare his teacher Husserl and concludes with the radical thesis that "philosophy can find its way back into its fundamental problems less than ever as long as it is primarily conceived on the model of the idea of a rigorous scientificality."[14]

3. In an introduction added in 1949 to the lecture "What Is Metaphysics?" under the title "The Way Back into the Ground of Metaphysics," and in the 1964 lecture "The End of Philosophy and the Task of Thinking," Heidegger attempts to come to terms once and for all with the problem of metaphysics. Metaphysics is immediately defined here through the forgetting of Being in the name of and in favor of beings: "Wherever the question is asked what beings are, beings as such are in sight. Metaphysical representation owes this sight to the light of Being. The light itself, i.e., that which such thinking experiences as light, no longer comes within the range of metaphysical thinking; for metaphysics always represents beings only as beings. [. . .] Because metaphysics interrogates beings as beings, it remains concerned with beings and does not turn itself to Being as Being."[15] Picking up the image from Descartes' letter to Picot with which the introduction begins, this is about thinking the ground – Being – in which philosophy casts its metaphysical roots. "The ground is ground for the roots," but the roots, qua roots, do not turn toward the ground and "forget themselves for the sake of the tree." This is why a mode of thinking that seeks to restore metaphysics and to think being rather than just being qua being cannot but somehow abandon metaphysics (*die Metaphysik in gewisser Weise verlassen*).[16] What is at issue for this kind of thinking is the overcoming of metaphysics: "When we think the truth

of Being, metaphysics is overcome [*überwunden*]. We can no longer accept the claim of metaphysics to preside over our fundamental relation to 'Being' or to decisively determine every relation to beings as such."[17] It is significant that the urgency of this overcoming is immediately tempered and that the syntagm is placed in scare quotes: "But this 'overcoming of metaphysics' does not abolish metaphysics. As long as man remains the *animal rationale*, he is the *animal metaphysicum*. As long as man understands himself as the rational animal, metaphysics belongs, as Kant said, to the nature of man. But if our thinking should succeed in its efforts to go back into the ground of metaphysics, it might well help to bring about a change in the human essence, a change accompanied by a transformation of metaphysics."[18]

By moving back toward this foundation, Heidegger once again confronts the dual configuration of early Aristotelian philosophy. "Metaphysics states what beings are as beings. [. . .] But metaphysics represents the beingness of beings in a twofold manner [*in zwiefacher Weise*]: in the first place, the totality of beings as such with an eye to their most universal traits (*on katholou, koinon*); but at the same time also the totality of beings as such in the sense of the highest and therefore divine being (*on katholou, akrotaton, theion*). In the metaphysics of Aristotle, the unconcealedness of beings as such has specifically developed in this twofold manner. Because it represents beings as beings, metaphysics is, in a twofold and yet unitary manner [*zwiefach-einig*], the truth of beings in their universality and in the highest being. According to its essence, metaphysics is at the same time both ontology in the narrower sense, and theology. This ontotheological essence of philosophy proper (*prōtē philosophia*) must indeed be grounded in the way in which the *on* opens up in it, namely, as *on*. Thus the theological character of ontology is not merely due to the fact that Greek metaphysics was later taken up and transformed by the ecclesiastic theology of Christianity. Rather it is due to the manner in which beings as beings have revealed themselves from early on. [. . .] As the truth of beings as such, metaphysics has a twofold character. The reason for this twofoldness, however, let alone its origin, remains closed to metaphysics; and this is no accident, nor due to mere neglect. Metaphysics has this twofold character because it is what it is: the representation of beings as beings. Metaphysics has no choice. As metaphysics, it is by its very essence excluded from the experience of Being."[19]

For this reason, even the "fundamental ontology" that in *Being and Time* defined the belonging-together of *Da-sein*[20] and being is, at this point, declared insufficient. "As long as this thinking calls itself 'fundamental ontology' it blocks and obscures its own path by this very designation. For what the title 'fundamental ontology' suggests is that the thinking that attempts to think the truth of being – and not, like all ontology, the truth of beings – is, as fundamental ontology, still a kind of ontology."[21]

4. The problem of "the onto-theological constitution of metaphysics" is at the heart of the eponymous lecture given in Todtnauberg, on February 25, 1957, at the close of a seminar on Hegel. Heidegger asks: "How does the deity enter into philosophy, not just modern philosophy, but philosophy as such?"[22] Since the deity can enter into philosophy only if philosophy

in its very essence demands it to step in, the question immediately translates into another: "What is the origin of the onto-theological constitution of metaphysics?" To ask this question in the context of Hegel's thought means situating it in a dimension in which being is conceived of as thought and onto-theology consequently presents itself as onto-theo-logics. Thus, if metaphysics becomes in Hegel the "science of logic," this is because being is revealed in the form of the logos and the logos is understood as the ground. This intertwining between logos and ground is where the deity makes its entrance into philosophy: "Being shows itself in the nature of the ground. Accordingly, the matter of thinking, Being as the ground, is thought out fully only when the ground is represented as the first ground, as *prōtē archē*. The original question of thinking presents itself as the original thing [*Ur-sache*, primal matter], the *causa prima* [. . .]. The Being of beings is represented fundamentally, in the sense of the ground, only as *causa sui*. This is the metaphysical concept of God."[23] Even though Heidegger does not name Aristotelian and medieval metaphysics, this divine metaphysical figure extends well beyond Hegelian ontology: "Man can neither pray nor sacrifice to this god. Before the *causa sui*, man can neither fall to his knees in awe nor can he play music and dance before this god."[24]

In contrast to this metaphysical paradigm, in which being and God are simply logical figures, Heidegger seeks to think being starting from the difference between Being and beings – a difference that, in metaphysics, remains unthought. "Metaphysics responds to Being as *logos*, and is accordingly in its basic characteristics everywhere logic, but a logic that thinks of the Being of beings, and thus the logic which is determined by what differs in the difference: onto-theo-logic. Since metaphysics thinks of beings as such as a whole, it represents beings in respect of what differs in the difference, and without heeding the difference as difference. What differs shows itself as the Being of beings in general, and as the Being of beings in the Highest."[25]

To find a way out of the onto-theological constitution of metaphysics, to think of difference as what it is, means to instead think *Austrag* (perdurance, sustainment): the mutual decision of Being and beings, their intersection and "circling . . . around each other."[26]

5. At this point we can try to define the radical strategy that Heidegger applies to metaphysics. He replaces the split in first philosophy between being qua being and the divine with an even earlier split, between Being and beings (the ontological difference). Thus the object of philosophy remains split and, while Heidegger's later thought attempts specifically to resolve it, it remains doubtful at best whether he succeeded in overcoming it. In his 1957 lecture the focus for thought is *Austrag*, the circular relationship between Being and beings, but in his 1964 lecture "The End of Philosophy and the Task of Thinking" thought beyond metaphysics is concerned with the clearing (*die Lichtung*) and the open (*das Offene*), terms that apparently take the place of Being in his later thought. And yet a radical figure of Being in its difference from beings is still at issue here. This becomes clear from the title he proposes at the end of the lecture for the task of thought, to take the place of *Being and Time*: "Clearing and Presence" (*Lichtung und Anwesenheit*).[27] "Presence" names ancient Greek

---

understanding of being qua being, and "clearing" is now the figure most proper to Being.

It is significant that the task of thinking announced in the "Time and Being" lecture is an attempt to think Being without beings: "We want to say something about the attempt to think Being without regard to its being grounded in terms of beings. The attempt to think Being without beings becomes necessary because otherwise, it seems to me, there is no longer any possibility of explicitly bringing into view the Being of what is today all over the earth."[28] The difficulty of resolving the split in the object of thought is demonstrated in the Postscript added to the fourth (1943) and fifth (1949) editions of "What Is Metaphysics?." In the text of the fourth edition, it was stated imperatively that "it belongs to the truth of Being that Being is certainly [*wohl*, probably, no doubt] without beings," whereas the fifth edition changes *wohl* to *nie*: "that being is never without beings."[29] The attempt (*Versuch*: this is just a trial and an experiment) to think Being "without" beings necessarily stems from the split he is trying to resolve. It is no less significant that in "The End of Philosophy and the Task of Thinking" the One that the term *Lichtung* names is defined as an *Ursache*, a "primal matter" or "original thing" (the same term used for the first cause in the 1957 lecture), in which all that comes into presence has "the place that gathers and protects everything."[30] The risk here is that the open, despite Heidegger's caution, will itself become a "thing," a kind of architranscendental, distinct once again from things and from the *res ratae* that come into presence in it.

---

6. It comes as no surprise, then, that the problem of the relationship between metaphysics and the sciences re-emerges powerfully at the beginning of the lecture and that the end of philosophy is closely linked to emancipating the regions of knowledge. "The development of the sciences is at the same time their separation from philosophy and the establishment of their independence. This process belongs to the completion of philosophy. [...] The development of philosophy into the independent sciences which, however, interdependently communicate among themselves ever more markedly, is the legitimate completion of philosophy. Philosophy is ending in the present age. [...] The sciences are now taking over as their own task what philosophy in the course of its history tried to present in part, and even there only inadequately, that is, the ontologies of the various regions of beings (nature, history, law, art). [...] However, the sciences still speak about the Being of beings in the unavoidable supposition of their regional categories. They just don't say so. They can deny their origin from philosophy, but never dispense with it. For in the scientific attitude of the sciences, the document of their birth from philosophy still speaks."[31] The question of whether there is another task for philosophy outside the decomposition of philosophy into the technicalized sciences – a question Heidegger asks at this point – remains unanswered in the second part of his lecture, which develops the theme of *Lichtung* and the open, without ever relating it to that of scientific disciplines.

To the extent that the object of philosophy remains somehow caught in the ontological difference, and therefore somehow split (or, put differently, if the opening is still a radical figure of Being), it cannot but border on the nothing, even in its separation from beings that Heidegger seeks to think – just as the transcendental "thing" is, in the end, only a not-thing. For this reason, the object of philosophy can only open the way for the particular sciences, to which it must ultimately yield its primacy once again. Similarly, since knowledge of beings separate from Being (knowledge of phenomena separate from the noumenon) has divided its object into two, as it were, from the beginning, then, far from opening the way to true science (as Kant believed in his critique of metaphysics), it can only end in a pseudoscience that renounces knowing the real in order to act upon it.

What must be called into question each time is the original splitting of the object of thought – into Being and beings, the existent and the thing, being and God, the transcendental and the empirical – which philosophy has failed to resolve. What remains to be thought, in Hölderlin's words, is that "every thing [. . .] is knowable in the medium (*moyen*) of its appearance, that the way in which it is conditioned [*bedingt*, lit. reduced to a thing] can be determined and taught."[32] Once again, philosophy must choose to leave behind both being and its transcendental stronghold to think a thing that is never separable from its openness and an open that is never separable from the thing. And only a knowledge that sets out to know a thing exclusively in the medium of its openness would be worthy of the name of science.

7. In any case, as long as the object of thought remains divided, knowledge in the West cannot but split into a plurality of sciences, whose unification will always remain problematic, even when its completion is

attempted through a theory that, as its name suggests, has a purely technical, pragmatic purpose ("cybernetics" is merely the art of the pilot who steers the sciences and does not posit any effective community between them). Being should have guaranteed the unity of knowledge, but, in the form of the transcendental, it can only deliver itself to the particular sciences, in which it is dismembered and compartmentalized to the same degree that it seeks to limit them. The ambiguity and dimorphism of being and thing – always already split into being and essence, *res rata* and *res a reor* – is destined to produce that oscillation from one extreme to the other that neither the Kantian critique nor Heidegger's fundamental ontology manages to dampen. From this perspective, metaphysics is the unrelenting transcendental illusion that leads philosophers time after time to take meaning for denotation and the transcendental object = X for a real being. The validity of the disciplines that metaphysics assigns to the West as its fate is founded, purely and precisely, on the incessant disenchantment of this illusion – and so is the separation of being from beings that legitimizes the regionalization of ontology according to the multiplicity of the sciences. It is in its inevitable errancy that metaphysics constitutes the foundation of western knowledge, and it is only the metaphysician's illusion that guarantees the scientist's objectivity. Until this secret nexus uniting metaphysics and science is clarified, the relationship between philosophy and the sciences will continue to be problematic. And this aporetic situation can be resolved only on condition that philosophy surrenders its primacy to make itself last instead of first – last not because it comes later, but

because at every turn it finds itself exposed and histori-
cally decided upon before the extreme fortunes of the
animal metaphysicum.

We all remember the episode in Cervantes' novel (I, 21) when
Don Quixote mistakes a barber's basin for the helmet of
Mambrino. In response to Sancho, who points out to his master
that the helmet is the spitting image of a good barber's basin, the
knight observes, as proof of the "oscillating reality" of his world,
that this "enchanted helmet, by some strange accident, must have
fallen into the hands of one who could not recognize or estimate
its value and [. . .] he must have melted down one half to take
advantage of its high price, and from the other half he made this,
which resembles a barber's basin, as you say." Don Quixote is
perfectly aware, then, that the heroic armor he promptly places
on his head looks like a barber's basin; nonetheless, he declares
that "the transformation makes no difference." As suggested by
the adjective "enchanted," which here makes its first unexpected
appearance, reality is oscillating because everything is being
counterfeited continuously by sorcerers and necromancers. "[A]ll
things having to do with knights errant," explains Don Quixote
to Sancho in one of the most philosophical dialogues in the novel,
"appear to be chimerical, foolish, senseless, and turned inside
out" because "hordes of enchanters always walk among us and
alter and change everything and turn things into whatever they
please, according to whether they wish to favor us or destroy
us; and so, what seems to you a barber's basin seems to me the
helmet of Mambrino, and will seem another thing to someone
else." The subtlety of this argument should not be overlooked.
Not only does the enchantment make it impossible to distinguish
a helmet from a basin, but the spell could ultimately prove ben-
eficial, by turning the knight and the enchanter back into allies:
"It was rare foresight on the part of the wise man who favors me
to make what is really and truly the helmet of Mambrino seem a
basin to everyone else, because it is held in such high esteem that
everyone would pursue me in order to take it from me; but since
they see it as only a barber's basin, they do not attempt to obtain
it." The chimeras of the knight errant are truly "turned inside

out," and what appeared to be madness is revealed in the end to be a special form of wisdom.

The philosopher can be compared to Don Quixote. Philosophers have before them an enchanted world in which people group themselves into squires, who, like Sancho and the scientists, see basins in the place of helmets, and knights errant, who, like the metaphysicians, want at all costs to recognize famous helmets in barbers' basins. Metaphysics, then (just like "all earnestness, all passion, and everything men take to heart," in the words of Nietzsche in a letter of December 8, 1875 to his friend Rohde) is "Quixotism" (*Don Quixoterie*): in certain cases it is good to be aware of it, "otherwise it is better not to know about it."[33] The helmet of Mambrino is being, which the metaphysical hidalgo "of old, at present, and always" searches for in particular things. In the enchanted eyes of humans, however, being has the risky tendency of reifying itself into basins and other barber's tools. Thought is poised between two enchantments: in every instance and almost in the same act, it must disenchant Sancho's basin and disprove Don Quixote's chimera – at the cost of finding itself, like the "dry and wrinkled" hidalgo, with his books of chivalry, and like Kant's metaphysician, lost "in a broad and stormy ocean [. . .], where many a fog bank and rapidly melting iceberg pretend to be new lands and, ceaselessly deceiving with empty hopes the voyager looking around for new discoveries, entwine him in adventures from which he can never escape and yet also never bring to an end."[34] The supreme object of metaphysics, which "always leads us into a dead-end" and yet we cannot help looking for it, consists solely in this twofold movement, like Pulcinella's disciplined gags or Don Quixote's cunning reveries.

Notes

Notes to Chapter 1

1 Foucault, pp. XV–XVI.
2 Simplicius, 1, 17–21; p. 39 in the English translation.
3 Alexander of Aphrodisias, p. 369.
4 *Metaphysics* E, 1026a24ff.; *Metaphysics* K, 1061b19; *Physics*, 192a35–36; *Physics*, 194b14–15; *On the Heavens*, 277b10; *On the Soul*, 403b16; *Movement of Animals*, 700b9; to which we must add *Metaphysics* Γ 1004a3–4.
5 Guyomarc'h, p. 145.
6 Ibid., p. 143.
7 Robin, p. 154.
8 Natorp, p. 49.
9 Ibid.
10 Aubenque, p. 38.
11 Brisson, p. 49.
12 Mansion, p. 180.
13 Ibid., p. 209.
14 Avicenna, p. 18.
15 Ibid., p. 14.

16 Ibid., p. 15.

17 Ibid., p. 17.

18 *On the Heavens*, 26a31: *ousia theiotera kai protera*; 279a35: *theioteron*; 292b22: *theiotatē archē*; Metaphysics 982b32: *theiotatē kai timiōtatē*; and in the adverbial form (Metaphysics 1074b10: *theiōs*).

19 Heidegger, 1980b, p. 190; p. 146 in the English translation.

20 Goldschmidt, p. 142.

21 Heidegger 1993, p. 269; p. 150 in the English translation.

22 Benveniste, p. 82; p. 57 in the English translation.

23 Boehm, p. 169.

24 Bubner, p. 180.

25 Alexander of Aphrodisias, p. 573.

26 Ibid., p. 571. See Robin, pp. 155–157.

27 Melandri, p. 10.

28 Guyomarc'h, p. 143.

29 [Translator's note: The word *moirai* (μοῖραι) is related to the words *meros* (part) and *moros* (fate). It is thought to come from the Proto-Indo-European root *mer-, which means "to divide" or "to share."]

Notes to Chapter 2

1 Boethius 1918, pp. 8 (Latin) and 9 (English).

2 Fidora, p. 695.

3 Gundissalinus, p. 15.

4 Ibid., p. 38.

5 Ibid.

6 Ibid., p. 37.

7 Ibid., pp. 36–37.

8 Ibid., p. 36.

9 Ibid., p. 5.

10 Ibid.
11 Ibid., p. 129.
12 Ibid., pp. 129–130.
13 Zimmermann, pp. 236–237.
14 Ibid.
15 Duns Scotus 1891–1895, p. 32a, n. 40; p. 51 in the English translation.
16 Ibid., p. 36a, n. 47; p. 57 in the English translation.

Notes to Chapter 3
 1 Pouillon, p. 42.
 2 Ibid., p. 43.
 3 Ventimiglia, pp. 219, 214.
 4 Armando di Belloviso (Armand de Belvézer), p. 319.
 5 Aubenque, p. 204.
 6 Courtine, p. 347.
 7 Avicenna, pp. 106–107.
 8 Ibid., p. 108.
 9 Ibid.
10 Ibid.
11 Gilson, p. 114.
12 Avicenna, p. 108.
13 Ibid., p. 110. See p. 27 in the English translation:

> (19) Hence, you have now understood the way in which "the thing" differs from what is understood by "the existent" and "the realized" and that, despite this difference, the two [that is, "the thing" and "the existent"] are necessary concomitants. (20) Yet, it has reached me that some people say that what is realized is realized without being an existent, that the description of a thing can be something neither existing nor nonexisting, and that the [expressions] "that which"

and "whichever" denote something other than that which [the expression] "the thing" denotes. Such people are not among the assemblage of the discerning.

14 De Libera, p. 583.

15 Bonaventura da Bagnoregio, p. 876.

16 Oeing-Hanhoff, pp. 285–295.

17 Folger-Fonfara, p. 39.

18 Henry of Ghent, 1991, qq. 1–2.

19 Aertsen, p. 288.

20 Courtine, p. 184.

21 Henry of Ghent, 1520, q. 3, a. 24, fol. 138vo.

22 Henry of Ghent, 1991, q. 9, ff. 465–466.

23 Demange p. 31.

24 Duns Scotus, 1891–1895, pp. 4–5.

25 Courtine, p. 139.

26 Duns Scotus, 1954, d. 3, p. 2, n. 311.

27 Ibid., d. 3, p. 2, n. 81.

28 Ibid.

29 Ibid.

30 Buridan, l. 4, q. V, f. 16.

31 Biard, p. 54.

32 Buridan, l. 4, q. 5, f. 16.

33 Clauberg, § 152, p. 195.

34 Ibid., § 2, p. 37.

35 Ibid., § 4, p. 2.

36 Courtine, p. 537.

37 Boulnois, p. 513.

38 Courtine, p. 535.

39 Baumgarten, § 1, p. 1.

40 Demange, p. 28.

41 Ibid.

Notes to Chapter 4

1 Ventimiglia, p. 219.
2 Ibid., p. 215.
3 Bacon, p. 224; p. 62 in the English translation.
4 Ventimiglia, p. 217.
5 Albert the Great, 1, q. 24, ch. 3.
6 Heidegger 1978, p. 119; p. 94 in the English translation.
7 Ibid., p. 114; p. 91 in the English translation.
8 Costabel and Redondi, p. 187.
9 Crapulli, p. 161.
10 Ibid., p. 162.
11 Ibid., p. 165.
12 Ibid., p. 163.
13 Ibid., p. 170.
14 Klein, p. 154.
15 Petrus Hispanus, p. 57.
16 Ockham, pp. 177–178; pp. 190–191 in the English translation.
17 Duns Scotus 1954, d. 3, p. 1, q. 2, no. 16; p. 44 in the English translation (Duns Scotus 2016).
18 Boethius, *On Aristotle, On Interpretation* (*In Peri hermeneias*), 2, 33, 27; p. 32 in the English translation (Boethius 2010), p. 32.
19 Ockham, p. 8; p. 49 in the English translation.
20 Ibid., p. 39; p. 74 in the English translation.
21 Ibid.
22 Paqué, p. 261.
23 Demange, p. 4.
24 Priscian, p. 552.
25 Macrobius, p. 271.
26 Duns Scotus 1954, d. 3, p. 3, n. 388.
27 Ibid., n. 386.

28 Ibid., n. 400.
29 Alnwick, p. 44.
30 Dilthey, p. 510; p. 231 in the English translation.
31 Kant 1977, p. 117.
32 Dilthey, p. 518; p. 237 in the English translation.
33 Dilthey, p. 238 in the English edition.

Notes to Chapter 5

 1 Kant 1960a, p. 13; p. 101 in the English translation.
 2 Ibid., p. 14; p. 102 in the English translation.
 3 Ibid., p. 16; p. 103 in the English translation.
 4 Ibid., p. 62; p. 132 in the English translation.
 5 Ibid., p. 46; p. 137 in the English translation.
 6 Ibid., p. 63; p. 133 in the English translation.
 7 Ibid., p. 64; p. 133 in the English translation.
 8 Ibid., p. 101; p. 196 in the English translation.
 9 Ibid., p. 276; p. 346 in the English translation.
10 Ibid.
11 Ibid., p. 275; p. 345 in the English translation.
12 Ibid.
13 Ibid., p. 280; p. 348 in the English translation.
14 Ibid., p. 281; p. 349 in the English translation.
15 Ibid., p. 277; p. 360 in the English translation.
16 Ibid., p. 276; p. 386 in the English translation.
17 Ibid., p. 310; p. 386 in the English translation.
18 Ibid., p. 311; p. 386 in the English translation.
19 Ibid., p. 387 in the English translation.
20 Ibid., p. 276; p. 345 in the English translation.
21 Ibid., pp. 275–276; p. 360 in the English translation.
22 Leisegang, p. 404.
23 Kant 1960a, p. 124; p. 217 in the English translation.
24 Kant 1977, p. 117 (English translation only).
25 Ibid., p. 118 (English translation only).

---

26 Ibid., p. 120 (English translation only).

27 Kant 1960a, p. 307; pp. 382–383 in the English translation.

28 Ibid., p. 284; p. 352 in the English translation.

29 Ibid., p. 11; p. 99 in the English translation.

30 Ibid., p. 282; p. 350 in the English translation.

31 Ibid.; p. 351 in the English translation.

32 Ibid., p. 267; p. 354 in the English translation.

33 Kant 1960b, pp. 12–13; p. 5 in the English translation.

34 Kant 1960a, p. 24; p. 114 in the English translation.

35 Fichte, p. 9; p. 162 in the English translation.

36 Ibid., p. 16; p. 166–67 in the English translation.

37 Ibid., p. 21; p. 170 in the English translation.

38 Ibid., p. 27; p. 174 in the English translation.

39 Ibid., p. 21; p. 170 in the English translation.

40 Ibid., p. 22; p. 171 in the English translation.

41 Ibid.

Notes to Chapter 6

1 Heidegger 1992, p. 250; p. 153 in the English translation.

2 Ibid.

3 Ibid.

4 Ibid.; p. 154 in the English translation.

5 Ibid., p. 252; p. 154 in the English translation.

6 Ibid., p. 239; p. 145 in the English translation.

7 Heidegger 1993, p. 409; pp. 227 and 240 in the English translation.

8 Ibid., p. 410; p. 227 in the English translation.

9 Heidegger 1990, p. 29; p. 14 in the English translation.

10 Ibid., p. 186; p. 156 in the English translation. [Translator's note: Here I maintain the lowercase 'b' for 'being' as preferred by the translator of Heidegger's

The *Metaphysical Foundations of Logic*, Michael Heim; see Translator's Afterword in that book, p. 230.]

11 Heidegger 1980a, p. 153; p. 100 in the English translation.

12 Heidegger 1975, p. 38; p. 29 in the English translation.

13 Heidegger 1980a, pp. 38–9; p. 10 in the English translation.

14 Ibid., pp. 38–9; p. 12 in the English translation.

15 Heidegger 1978, pp. 361–2; pp. 277–8 in the English translation (Heidegger 1998).

16 Ibid., p. 363; p. 278 in the English translation (Heidegger 1998).

17 Ibid.; p. 279 in the English translation (Heidegger 1998).

18 Ibid.

19 Ibid., pp. 373–4; pp. 288–9 in the English translation (Heidegger 1998).

20 [Translator's note: I hyphenate *Da-sein* here in accordance with Joan Stambaugh's remark in her translator's preface to *Being and Time*: "It was Heidegger's express wish that in future translations the word *Da-sein* should be hyphenated throughout *Being and Time*." Heidegger 1996, p. xiv]

21 Ibid., p. 375; p. 289 in the English translation (Heidegger 1998).

22 Heidegger 2006, p. 67; p. 55 in the English translation.

23 Ibid.; pp. 56, 59–60 in the English translation.

24 Ibid., p. 77; p. 72 in the English translation.

25 Ibid., p. 76; p. 70 in the English translation.

26 Ibid., p. 75; p. 69 in the English translation.

27 Heidegger 2007, p. 89; p. 449 in the English translation. This is the essay "The End of Philosophy and the Task of Thinking," in Heidegger 1977.

28 Ibid., p. 5; this is the essay "Time and Being," and the version given here is from Heidegger 1972 (which is a series of conference papers).

29 Heidegger 1978, p. 304; translated here from the Italian.

30 Heidegger 2007, p. 81; pp. 442–3 in the English translation.

31 Ibid., pp. 72–3; pp. 57–9 in the English translation (Heidegger 1972).

32 Hölderlin, p. 195; p. 101 in the English translation.

33 Nietzsche, p. 106.

34 Kant, 1960a; p. 354 in the English translation.

References

Aertsen, J. *Medieval Philosophy as Trascendental Thought: From Philip the Chancellor to Francisco Suarez*. Leiden-Boston: Brill, 2012.

Albert the Great. *Summa theologiae, sive de mirabili scientia Dei*, edited by D. Siedler, in *Alberti Magni Opera omnia*, vol. 34. Münster: Aschendorff, 1978.

Alexander of Aphrodisias. *Commentario alla Metafisica di Aristotele*, edited by G. Movia. Milan: Bompiani, 2007. For some quotations, see the English renderings in Mirjam E. Kotwick, *Alexander of Aphrodisias and the Text of Aristotle's* Metaphysics. Berkeley: California Classical Studies, 2016.

Alnwick, G. *Guillelmi Alnwick Quaestiones disputatae de esse intelligibili et de Quodlibet*, edited by P. A. Ledoux. Florence: Quaracchi, 1937.

Armando di Belloviso. *Declaratio difficilium terminorum theologiae, philosophiae atque logicae Armandi Bellovisii*. Venice: Aldus, 1586.

Aubenque, P. *Le problème de l'être chez Aristote*. Paris: PUF, 1966.

References

Avicenna. *La Métaphysique su Shifa'*, books 1–5, translated into French by G. C. Anawati. Paris: Vrin, 1978.

All references to page numbers are to this volume.

For the text of the translation into Latin, see *Avicenna latinus: Liber de philosophia prima sive scientia divina*, edited by S. Van Riet. Louvain-Leiden: Brill, 1977–83, 3 vols.

For the original Arabic text with an English translation, see *The Metaphysics of* The Healing, translated, introduced, and annotated by Michael E. Marmura. Provo, UT: Brigham Young University Press, 2005.

Bacon, R. *Summulae dialectices*. In A. de Libera, *Les Summulae dialectices de Roger Bacon*. Paris: Vrin, 1986, pp. 132–289.

English translation consulted: *The Art and Science of Logic*, translated by Thomas S. Maloney. Toronto: Pontifical Institute of Medieval Studies, 2009.

Baumgarten, A. G. *Metaphysica*, Halle, Madeburg: C. H. Hemmerde, 1739.

Benveniste, É. *Problèmes de linguistique générale*. Paris: Gallimard, 1966.

English translation used: *Problems in General Linguistics*, translated by Mary Elizabeth Meeks. Coral Gables: University of Miami Press, 1971.

Biard, J. "L'analyse logique des termes transcendantaux 'chez Jean Buridan," in G. Federici Vescovini, ed., *Le Problème des transcendantaux du XIVᵉ au XVIIᵉ siècle*. Paris: Vrin, 2002, pp. 50–66.

Boehm, R. *Das Grundlegende und das Wesentliche: Aristoteles' Abhandlung "Über das Sein und das Seiende" (Metaphysik Z)*. The Hague: Nijhoff, 1965.

Boethius. *On the Trinity*, in *Theological Tractates and*

References

The Consolation of Philosophy (bilingual Latin–English edition), edited by H. F. Stewart and E. K. Rand, Cambridge, MA: Havard University Press, 1968, pp. 2–31.

Boethius. *On Aristotle, On interpretation 1–3*, translated by Andrew Smith. London: Bloomsbury, 2010.

Bonaventura da Bagnoregio. *Commentarius in II librum Sententiarum*, in *Opera omnia*, vol. 2. Quaracchi Friars, Florence: ex Typographia Collegii S. Bonaventurae, 1885.

Boulnois, O. *Être et représentation: Une généalogie de la métaphysique moderne à l'epoque de Duns Scot (XIIIᵉ-XIVᵉ siècles)*. Paris: PUF, 1999.

Brentano, F. *Von der mannigfachen Bedeutung des Seienden nach Aristoteles*. Freiburg: Herder, 1862.

> Italian translation used: F. Brentano, *Sui molteplici significati dell'essere secondo Aristotele*, edited by G. Reale, translated by S. Tognoli. Milan: Vita e Pensiero, 1995.

Brisson, L. "Un si long anonymat," in J.-M. Narbonne and L. Langlois, eds, *La Métaphysique: Son histoire, sa critique, ses enjeux*. Paris/Québec: Vrin/Presses de l'Université Laval-Québec, 1999, pp. 37–60.

Bubner, R, "Aristoteles oder die Geburt der Ontologie aus dem Geist der Sprache," *Philosophische Rundschau*, 24.314 (1977), pp. 177–186.

Buridan, G. *In Metaphysicen Aristotelis quaestiones argutissimae*. Paris: Badius, 1518.

Cervantes, M. *Don Quixote*, translated by Edith Grossman, introduction by Harold Bloom. New York: Harper-Collins, 2005.

Clauberg, J. *Elementa Philosophiae sive Ontosophia*. Groningen: ex Typis Johannis Nicolai, 1647.

References

Costabel, P., and Redondi, P. "Contribution à la semantèse de res/cosa/cossa dans la langue scientiphique du XVIᵉ siècle," in *Res: Atti del III Colloquio Internazionale del Lessico Intellettuale Europeo*, edited by M. Fattori and M. Bianchi. Rome: Edizioni dell'Ateneo, 1982, pp. 179–196.

Courtine, J.-F. *Suarez et le système de la métaphysique.* Paris: PUF, 1990.

Crapulli, G. "'Res' e 'cosa' ("cossa") nella terminologia algebrica del secolo XVI," in *Res: Atti del III Colloquio Internazionale del Lessico Intellettuale Europeo*, edited by M. Fattori and M. Bianchi. Rome: Edizioni dell'Ateneo, 1982.

De Libera, A. *L'art des généralités.* Paris: Aubier, 1999.

Demange, D. "Métaphysique et théorie de la représentation: La question des origines du transcendantalisme revisitée." *Revue philosophique de Louvain* 107 (2009), 1, pp. 1–39.

Dilthey, W. *Einleitung in die Geisteswissenschaften*, in *Gesammelte Schriften*, vol. 1. Stuttgart/Göttingen: Teubner/Ruprecht, 1966.
  English translation used: *Introduction to the Human Sciences*, in *Selected Works*, vol. 1, edited by R. A. Makkreel and F. Rodi. Princeton, NJ: Princeton University Press, 1989.

Duns Scotus, J. *Quaestiones super libros Metaphysicorum Aristotelis*, vol. 7 of *Opera omnia* (12 vols). Paris: Vivès, 1891–1895.
  English translation consulted: Duns Scotus, *Questions on the Metaphysics of Aristotle: Books One–Five*, translated by Girard J. Etzkorn and Allan B. Wolter. St. Bonaventure, NY: Franciscan Institute Publications, 1997.

References

Duns Scotus, J. *Ordinatio: Liber primus*, vol. 3 of *Ioannis Duns Scoti Opera omnia*. Civitas Vaticana, 1954.
English translation used: *On Being and Cognition: Ordinatio 1.3*, edited and translated by John van den Bercken. New York: Fordham University Press, 2016.

Fichte, G. A. *Grundlage der gesammten Wissenschaftslehre*. Leipzig: Gabler, 1794–1795.
English translation used: "Concerning the Concept of the Wissehschaftslehre," in *Foundation of the Entire Wissenschaftslehre and Related Writings (1794–1795)*, translated and edited by Daniel Breazeale. Oxford: Oxford University Press, 2021.

Henry of Ghent. *Summa quaestionum ordinarium theologicae*, vol. 1. Paris: Badius, 1520.

Henry of Ghent. *Quodlibet VII*, in *Henrici de Gandavo Opera omnia*, edited by G. A. Wilson, vol. 11. Leuven: Leuven University Press, 1991.

Fidora, A. "Dominicus Gundissalinus and the Introduction of Metaphysics into the Latin World," *Review of Metaphysics* 66.4 (2013), pp. 691–712.

Folger-Fonfara, S. *Das "Super"-Transzendentale und die Spaltung der Metaphysik: Der Entwurf des Franziskus von Marchia*. Leiden: Brill, 2008.

Foucault, M. *Naissance de la clinique: Une archéologie du regard médical*. Paris: PUF, 1963.
English translation used: *The Birth of the Clinic: An Archaeology of Medical Perception*, translated by A. M. Sheridan. Abingdon: Routledge, 2003.

Gilson, É. "Avicenne et le point de départ de Duns Scot," *Archives d'histoire doctrinale et littéraire du Moyen Âge* 2 (1927), pp. 89–149.

Goldschmidt, V. "Theologia," in *Questions platoniciennes*. Paris: Vrin, 1970.

References

Gundissalinus. *De divisione philosophiae*, edited by L. Baur. Münster: Aschendorff, 1903.

Guyomarc'h, G. "Fonctions et objets de la 'philosophie première' chez Aristote," *Revue de philosophie ancienne* 23.2 (2014), pp. 137–178.

Heidegger, M. "Time and Being," translated by Joan Stambaugh, in *On Time and Being*. New York: Harper & Row, 1972, pp. 1–24.

Heidegger, M. *Die Grundprobleme der Phänomenologie*. Frankfurt: Klostermann, 1975.
English translation used: *The Basic Problems of Phenomenology*, translated by Albert Hofstadter. Bloomington and Indianapolis: Indiana University Press, 1988.

Heidegger, M. *Was ist Metaphysik?* In *Wegmarken*. Frankfurt: Klostermann, 1978.
English translation used: "What Is Metaphysics?" translated by David Farrell Krell, in *Pathmarks*, edited by William McNeill. Cambridge: Cambridge University Press, 1998, pp. 82–96.

Heidegger, M. *Hegels Phänomenologie des Geistes*. Frankfurt: Klostermann, 1980a.
English translation used: *Hegel's Phenomenology of Spirit*, translated by Parvis Emad and Kenneth Maly. Bloomington and Indianapolis: Indiana University Press, 1988.

Heidegger, M. "Hegels Begriff der Erfahrung," in *Holzwege*. Frankfurt: Klostermann, 1980b.
English translation used: "Hegel's Concept of Experience," in *Off the Beaten Track*, edited and translated by Julian Young and Kenneth Haynes. Cambridge: Cambridge University Press, 2002, pp. 86–156.

References

Heidegger, M. *Metaphysische Anfangsgründe der Logik*. Frankfurt: Klostermann, 1990.
English translation used: *The Metaphysical Foundations of Logic*, translated by Michael Heim. Bloomington and Indianapolis: Indiana University Press, 1984.

Heidegger, M. *Platon: Sophistes*. Frankfurt: Klostermann, 1992.
English translation used: *Plato's Sophist*, translated by Richard Rojcewicz and André Schuwer. Bloomington & Indianapolis: Indiana University Press, 1997.

Heidegger, M. *Die Grundbegriffe der antiken Philosophie*. Frankfurt: Klostermann, 1993.
English translation used: *Basic Concepts of Ancient Philosophy*, translated by Richard Rojcewicz. Bloomington and Indianapolis: Indiana University Press, 2008.

Heidegger, M. *Being and Time*, translated by Joan Stambaugh. Albany: State University of New York, 1996.

Heidegger, M. "Introduction to 'What Is Metaphysics?,'" in *Pathmarks*, translated by Walter Kaufmann, edited by William McNeill. Cambridge: Cambridge University Press, 1998, pp. 277–290.

Heidegger, M. *Identität und Differenz*. Frankfurt: Klostermann, 2006.
English translation used: "The Onto-Theological Constitution of Metaphysics," in *Identity and Difference* (2nd edn.), translated by Joan Stambaugh. Chicago, IL: University of Chicago Press, 2002, pp. 42–74.

Heidegger, M. *Zur Sache des Denkens*. Frankfurt: Klostermann, 2007.

References

English translation used: "The End of Philosophy and the Task of Thinking," translated by David Krell, in *Basic Writings*, New York: Haper & Row, 1977, pp. 431–449.

Hölderlin, F. *Sämtliche Werke*, vol. 5: *Übersetzungen*, edited by F. Beissner. Stuttgart: W. Kohlammer, 1954. English translation consulted: "Remarks on 'Oedipus,'" translated by Thomas Pfau, in *Essays and Letters on Theory*. New York: State University of New York Press, 1988.

Jaeger, W. *Aristoteles. Grundlegung einer Geschichte seiner Entwicklung*. Berlin: Weidmannsche Buchhandlung, 1923. English translation used: *Aristotle: Fundamentals of the History of His Development* (2nd edn.), translated by Richard Robinson. Oxford: Oxford University Press, 1968.

Kant, I. *Kritik der reinen Vernunft*, vol. 2 in *Werke in sechs Bänden*, edited by W. Weischedel. Leipzig: Insel Verlag, 1960a. English translation used: *Critique of Pure Reason*, edited and translated by Paul Guyer and Allen W. Wood. Cambridge: Cambridge University Press, 1998.

Kant, I. *Metaphysische Anfangsgründe der Naturwissenschaft*, vol. 5 in *Werke in sechs Bänden*, edited by W. Weischedel. Leipzig: Insel Verlag, 1960b. English translation used: *Metaphysical Foundations of Natural Science*, edited and translated by Michael Friedman. Cambridge: Cambridge University Press, 2004.

Kant, I. *Prolegomena to Any Future Metaphysics and Letter to Marcus Herz, February 1772*, translated by

References

James W. Ellington. Indianapolis, IN: Hackett Publishing Company, 1977.

Klein, J. "Die griechische Logistik und die Entstehung der Algebra" (Parts I and II), *Quellen und Studien zur Geschichte der Mathematik, Astronomie und Physik* 3.1 (1934), pp. 1–105 and 3.2 (1936), pp. 122–235. English translation used: *Greek Mathematical Thought and the Origin of Algebra*, translated by Eva Braun. Cambridge, MA: MIT Press, 1968.

Leisegang, H. "Über die Behandlung des scholastischen Satzes: "Quodlibet ens est unum, verum, bonum seu perfectum," und seine Bedeutung in Kants Kritik der reinen Vernunft," *Kant-Studien* 20.1–3 (1915), pp. 403–421.

Macrobius. *I Saturnali*, edited by N. Marinone. Turin: Utet, 1977. (The references to pages are to this volume.) English translation used: *Saturnalia*. Cambridge, MA Harvard University Press, 2011.

Maioli, B. *Gli universali: Alle origini del problema*. Rome: Bulzoni, 1973.

Mansion, A. "Philosophie première, philosophie seconde et métaphysique chez Aristote," *Revue philosophique de Louvain*, 50 (1958), pp. 169–221.

Melandri, E. *La linea e il circolo*. Macerata: Quodlibet, 2004.

Moraux, P. *Les listes anciennes des ouvrages d'Aristote*. Louvain: Éditions Universitaires, 1951.

Natorp, P. "Thema und Disposition der aristotelischen Metaphysik," *Philosophische Monatshefte* 24 (1888), pp. 37–65.

Nietzsche, F. *Selected Letters*, authorized translation by Anthony M. Ludovici. Garden City, New York: Doubleday, Page & Company, 1921.

Ockham, W. *Summa logicae*, Ph. Boehner, ed. Franciscan

References

Institute Publications, St. Bonaventure-Louvain-Padeborn, 1957.

English translation used: William of Ockham. *Ockham's Theory of Terms: Part I of the Summa Logicae*, translated and introduced by Michael J. Loux. University of Notre Dame Press, Notre Dame, Indiana, 1974.

Oeing-Hanhoff, L. "'Res' comme concept transcendantal et sur-transcendantal," in *Res: Atti del III Colloquio Internazionale del Lessico Intellettuale Europeo*, edited by M. Fattori and M. Bianchi. Rome: Edizioni dell'Ateneo, 1982.

Paqué, R. *Das pariser Nominalistenstatut: Zur Entstehung der Realitätsbegriffs der Neuzeitlichen Naturwissenschaft / Occam, Buridan, and Petrus Hispanus, Nikolaus von Autrecourt und Gregor von Rimini*. Berlin: De Gruyter, 1970.

Petrus Hispanus. *Petri Hispani Summulae logicales, quas e codice manu scripto Reg. Lat. 1205*, edited by I. M. Bochenski, Turin: Marietti, 1947.

Pouillon, H. "Le premier traité des propriétés transcendantales: La 'Summa de bono' du Chancelier Philippe," *Revue néoscolastique de philosophie*, 42.61 (1939), pp. 40–77.

Priscian. *Prisciani Grammatici Caesariensis Institutionum grammaticarum*, books 1–12, edited by M. Hertzius, in *Grammatici latini*, edited by H. Keilius, vol. 2. Leipzig: Teubner, 1855.

Ricoeur, P. *Being, Essence, and Substance in Plato and Aristotle*, translated by David Pellauer and John Starkey. Cambridge: Polity, 2013.

Robin, L. *La Théorie platonicienne des idées et des nombres d'après Aristote*. Paris: Alcan, 1908.

References

Simplicius. *In Aristotelis Physica commentaria*, edited by H. Diels, in *Commentaria in Aristotelem graeca*, vol. 9. Berlin: Reimer, 1882. E

    English translation used: Simplicius, *On Aristotle, Physics 1.1–2*, translated by Stephen Mann. London: Bloomsbury, 2022.

Ventimiglia, G. *Differenza e contraddizione: Il problema dell'essere in Tommaso d'Aquino*. Milan: Vita e Pensiero, 1997.

Zimmermann, A. *Ontologie oder Metaphysik? Die Diskussion über den Gegenstand der Metaphysik im 13. und 14. Jahrhundert*. Leiden-Köln: Brill, 1965.

Index

Index

Index

Index

Index

Index